Praise for *Mystery Manifest*

As I have come to expect of Gail Ramshaw's writing, her use of language in *Mystery Manifest* is both graceful and provocative: graceful in her steady exploration of image and word; provocative in the many questions she poses but does not answer throughout the book. She gently but persistently presses us—and press she does—to a deeper reading of scripture, fuller engagement with its varied figures of speech, and humble awareness of the inadequacy of all language in describing who God is for us.

—E. Byron (Ron) Anderson, Styberg Professor of Worship, Garrett-Evangelical Theological Seminary, Evanston, Illinois

There are very few, if any, scholars who are as equipped as Gail Ramshaw to address important questions around liturgical language, specifically questions that relate to gender. In this important book, Ramshaw provides us with a dazzling array of images, titles, and descriptions with regard to the three Persons of the Trinity, as well as the Trinity as such. She consistently provokes us into rethinking our categories and engaging in deeper thought. The many questions sprinkled throughout invite us into a conversation with her, with ourselves, and with others. I doubt there is anyone who will not be profoundly challenged by this work.

—John F. Baldovin, S.J., Clough School of Theology and Ministry, Boston College

No one opens up the way we tell the truth about God with figures of speech like Gail Ramshaw. At once an exposition of the ways we speak of God and a repeated invitation to consider what this range of figural speech calls out of us, this book will be invaluable to theologians, liturgical leaders, and catechists alike. This is Ramshaw's masterwork.

—James W. Farwell, professor of theology and liturgy, Virginia Theological Seminary and the General Theological Seminary, and author of *Ritual Excellence*

In *Mystery Manifest*, Gail Ramshaw invites the Christian church to embrace expansiveness in addressing, identifying, and understanding the character, identity, and nature of God through examining the names, metaphors, figures of speech, and descriptors we attach to the triune God. As a theologian, liturgist, and pastor who serves the National Ministries and a local church in the United Church of Christ, I find the value and potential uses of this resource in theological reflection, sermon preparation, Bible studies, and liturgical curation innumerable.

—Cheryl A. Lindsay, minister for worship and theology, United Church of Christ

One of the great observations in Gail Ramshaw's new book, *Mystery Manifest*, is that Christianity has no original language. Instead, it always has been and always must be translated. This point of view is universal, and even a pastor like me in Finland, a small Northern European country, using Finnish as a working language, can benefit from this book written in English about the language of faith and about the names we use for God. Every language and every generation must give the Christian faith a new translation, and this book helps us to do that.

We have a dilemma: it is impossible to speak of God in the precise way the Western society would prefer. Yet we have been called to speak and sing. To communicate our ideas or experiences of God, we must use images, parables, and figures of speech, and be satisfied with the obscure picture they paint, like a piece of art that changes when you take a step closer or further away.

Gail Ramshaw has written many remarkable books about the language of faith. This may be the most important one of them. For all, it is a treasury for many meditations and sermon preparations. Tolle, lege!

—Terhi Paananen, adviser for liturgy, worship, and spiritual life, Evangelical Lutheran Church of Finland

Gail Ramshaw's book is a treasury of biblical and church sources to think and speak about God the Trinity, from anthropomorphic to naturalistic to mythical figures of speech. Ramshaw argues persuasively that we need a community to recognize metaphorical intention in religious discourse, relying on more than words or sounds, but on images, gestures, and symbols to communicate divine mystery. After reading her book, the richness of the lectionary alone will acquire new meaning for you.

—Nelson Rivera, professor of theology and ethics, United Lutheran Seminary

This book's modest size veils a spacious vessel, containing in its hold a rich exploration into language used to address and describe God that builds upon the author's previous masterful works on the subject. Pithy annotations on the vast array of scriptural figures of speech for the three Persons of the Trinity, and indeed for the Three-In-One, are coupled with an inventive and wide-ranging selection of examples drawn from post-scriptural sources, both classic and contemporary. Ramshaw's navigation of cutting-edge topics in the rapidly moving field of language theory, such as essentialism and binary limitations, make this book not only a treasure trove of images to enrich liturgy and prayer but also a wise and timely guide to today's evolving questions regarding theology and language.

—Martin A. Seltz, publisher, *Evangelical Lutheran Worship*

MYSTERY MANIFEST

MYSTERY MANIFEST

THE TRIUNE GOD, FIGURATIVELY SPEAKING

GAIL RAMSHAW

Fortress Press
Minneapolis

MYSTERY MANIFEST
The Triune God, Figuratively Speaking

30 29 28 27 26 25 1 2 3 4 5 6 7 8 9

Library of Congress Control Number: 2024022179 (print)

Cover image: The Burning Bush/Daniel Nevins. All rights reserved. Used by permission. www.danielnevins.com
Cover design: Laurie Ingram

Print ISBN: 978-1-5064-9498-2
eBook ISBN: 978-1-5064-9499-9

CONTENTS

ACKNOWLEDGMENTS

WITH WHOLEHEARTED GRATITUDE, I acknowledge the gracious welcome extended to me by the Bishop Payne Library at the Virginia Theological Seminary in Alexandria, Virginia. Without my continual use of the library's extensive resources, I could not have written this book. My thanks goes also to my editor at Fortress Press, Laura Gifford, for her enthusiastic support and timely advice; to my project manager Lisa Eaton, for her careful and persistent work on my behalf; and to the Liturgical Language Seminar of the North American Academy of Liturgy, for its ongoing encouragement and helpful suggestions. And thank you, Gordon Lathrop, for all your assistance.

I offer this book with gratefulness, first to the memory of Julian of Norwich, who wrote in *A Revelation of Love* her extraordinary description of Christ as our mother, delighting in a figure of speech which took the churches over half a millennium to welcome, and to the many people who have encouraged my work, especially Stephen Burns and Kevin Strickland.

FOREWORD

Jesus used this figure of speech with them, but they did not understand what he was saying to them.

—John 10:6

WELCOME TO THE study of the figures of speech that Christians have used in the past and the present to invoke and describe the triune God.

Over the last century, many Christians have given considerable attention to the anthropomorphic imagery of God as father and, subsequently, of God as mother. Already in 1978 I joined this conversation, writing a master's essay on Lutheran liturgical prayer and God as mother.[1] Since then I have become interested in exploring Christians' countless images for God, many of which are not anthropomorphic but objective.[2] I have searched for these figures of speech in the Bible, patristic sermons, theological treatises, mystical reveries, liturgical texts, and hymns, as well as in poems written by Christians. In this book I present a summary of my mature thinking on this complex issue by citing and discussing over 250 figures of speech that Christians have used in invoking and describing the triune God.

Throughout this book, as if I am answering the repeated "What does this mean?" found in *Luther's Small Catechism*, I have often included not only explanatory comments but also interpretive reflections. These personal thoughts reflect the three sources of study that have most influenced my work. First, arising in the eighteenth century, critical biblical studies have been invaluable in indicating the original meaning of biblical expression and often in assisting the worshipers' appropriation of biblical language. Second, the twentieth-century scholarly examination of metaphor has revived interest in the pattern of Christian interpretation, found especially in the church fathers and medieval mystics. This reliance on metaphor is seen in the texts of many recent hymn writers, in which biblical metaphors have been expanded to embrace the worshipers' own time and place. Third, the feminist movement has taught me to make critical judgments about a tradition too often and too entirely focused on the male. Thus this book advocates the combining of critical biblical studies with contemporary imaginal spirituality and feminist analysis as the welcome technique when examining and composing language to and about God.

The title of this book recalls the King James translation of Colossians 1:26 that I memorized in my childhood, about "the mystery . . . now made manifest" to the faithful. God is beyond knowing, outside human speech: thus mystery. Yet Christians claim to have been given salvific access to that mystery. As more recent biblical translations have rendered this passage in Colossians, the divine mystery is revealed, disclosed, shown forth in the life, death, and resurrection of Jesus Christ. Since this mystery is thus to some degree "made manifest" through sacred wording, believers are called to honor Christian speech, to read the Scriptures, to attend to proclamation, to pray and sing the many classic figures of speech, and perhaps even to welcome expressions newly proposed by believers.

Thus chapters 1–2 discuss the various ways that words can manifest the mystery of God. Chapter 1 outlines the universal Christian practice of addressing and describing God through simile, metaphor, epithets, parables, and narratives, utilizing both anthropomorphic and objective figures of speech. Since a book dealing with all genres of figures of speech and every grammatical form would be impossibly lengthy, this study will focus on "is" nouns, words that are set parallel to "God." That is, this book will deal with nouns that believers claim can serve as partial explanatory equivalents: for example, God "the Father" suggests that "father" is in some ways an adequate descriptor of God, an appropriate figure of speech for the divine. Some of these appositives will be familiar to readers, some not—some welcomed, some not. Chapter 2 gives an example of our ongoing tasks of reflection and interpretation by exploring the somewhat rare figure of speech of God the Fire.

But the word *manifest* also means a listing of the cargo that is carried on board a ship. Believers have asserted that life on the ark of the church will be enhanced if we attend with care to the cargo we carry, and that cargo includes the vocabulary we use to articulate and convey our faith. Chapters 3–7 turn to lists and discussions of specific examples of figures of speech used by Christians to invoke and describe the Trinity; we can think of these lists as the manifest of the ship of the baptized. Some lists are set up alphabetically; other lists are ordered in some other appropriate manner. Chapter 3 focuses on the First Person of the Trinity, chapter 4 the Second Person of the Trinity, and chapter 5 the Third Person of the Trinity. Chapter 6 attends to triple formulations that refer to the whole Trinity, the Three-in-One. Since even our standard vocabulary of "Father" and "Son" utilizes figures of speech, this book tends to prefer First, Second, and Third Person as primary designations for our God. This book also capitalizes the term *Person*, as well as First, Second, and Third, when writing about the

Three-in-One, to highlight the uniquely theological meaning of this odd but traditional term when it is applied to the Trinity.

A consideration of Trinitarian titles and images by necessity must include attention to primary theological issues. So chapter 3 considers the Christian habit of valuing divine anthropomorphisms; chapter 4 focuses on the classic Christology that understands Jesus Christ as being of both divine and human nature; chapter 5 attends especially to the issue of divine gender; and chapter 6 examines the two patterns, traditionally called the "immanent" and the "economic," of naming the Three-in-One. Chapter 7 describes extended figures of speech and then discusses the ways that figures of speech actually function within the community of faith, especially at assembly worship.

> *From John Donne in the seventeenth century:*
>
> My God, my God, thou art a direct God, may I not say a literal God, a God that wouldst be understood literally and according to the plain sense of all that thou sayest? But thou art also a figurative, a metaphorical God, too: a God in whose words there is such a height of figures, such voyages, such peregrinations to fetch remote and precious metaphors, such extensions, such spreadings, such curtains of allegories, such third heavens of hyperboles, so harmonious elocutions, so retired and so reserved expressions, so commanding persuasions . . . thou art the Dove that flies.[3]

The box that here quotes John Donne is the first of many such boxes throughout the text, short passages that attend—concretely or obliquely—to the discussion at hand and that invite your consideration. Additionally, throughout the book, many paragraphs conclude with a question, inviting the reader to think beyond my text.

Please note a few preliminary comments: I am working in American English. Many quotations that I cite appeared first in another language. Given that alternative translations are available, the endnotes will indicate my source, as best as can be determined, for each non-biblical quote. All biblical citations will come from the NRSV translation of the Bible.

The word *god* is wider than Christianity, but in this book I will attend to its usage within Christianity and thus will capitalize it, trusting the noun to function without gender distinction. As a Christian, I affirm that from before time until the end of all things, this God is triune, active in each situation through one, two, or all three Persons of the Trinity.

Although this work cites many dozens of figures of speech for the triune God, I am not pretending that these lists are exhaustive. Indeed, Christians have been and continue to be remarkably creative in their language for God. To ensure that this volume does not become repetitive, I will attend usually only once to each figure of speech. The Index of Figures of Speech will assist the reader in locating the single or several places in which each figure appears.

Please join me on board the ship. I hope that you find the ship's manifest a blessing at Sunday worship and beyond. ***Question:*** *Is the Trinity the captain or the crew of our ship, or is God the Ship?*

1

FIGURES OF SPEECH, WHY AND WHERE

Literal Speech and God

THE WESTERN WORLD has valued precision in speaking, writing, and communicating. As a person formed in that Western world, schooled in its centuries of written texts, and adept at composition in at least contemporary American English, I am grateful to live in a society that hopes to thrive by continuing a tradition of accurate speech. When at times during recent centuries rational communication has broken down, when realities have fallen through the cracks into unlit basements below, when nonsense has been shouted out and accepted as truth, there remain many persons who persevere in maintaining literal and certifiable language. We might say that despite the disgruntled musicians who are spitting into their trumpets off stage, the orchestras can still drown out discordant noise with the coordinated music of correct notes and appropriate cadences. It is as if accurately spoken information is a welcome symphony to our ears.

There is of course always the danger that, as periodically has happened in the past, falsehoods and lies can sound more attractive than facts, that literal truth can be obscured by meaningless racket. It might be that sometime in the future the legacy of the Enlightenment comes to be rejected, its principles replaced by narrow and self-serving fantasies, the people preferring babble. But not yet. At least in my experience, it is still the case that an old woman walking to the market is not publicly hanged for causing communal chaos because she cursed her neighbor's cows. Western Christianity has benefited from this culture of accurate speech. The goal of billions of people over twenty centuries being able to participate in one worldwide community of Christian worship and care has meant that words have had to be crafted and translated and discussed and written and shared, words that suggest who God is and why this matters for persons struggling in a needy world. And although I cannot join him in each of his decisions about language, I remain grateful for Thomas Aquinas trying valiantly to fit into his brain both Aristotle and the Scriptures, searching for a single coherent religious system articulated in literally acceptable speech, and I agree with Aquinas that speaking devoutly about the triune God has never been easy.

Yet despite my debt to literal speech, my life's work has found its impetus by a religious tradition that included not only biblical narratives and theological discourses, but also mystics and hymn writers who called out, "Let's try to say it this way." As part of my eighth-grade preparation for confirmation and first communion, I had to memorize a description of God as "eternal, unchangeable, omnipotent, omniscient, omnipresent, holy, just, faithful, benevolent, merciful, and gracious."[1] Of this definition, I repeat what a friend has said about at least some inadequate chancel art, "Well, it's something to work with." And I have indeed worked with this tradition of words to and about God. Since in the church, despite various efforts toward ecclesiastical dictatorship, there has not been an unbreakable, unbreachable wall of authority; there has always been heard some new arrangement of words, some alternate way to speak about the Trinity and the actions of the triune God in our world. In our time, this search for the most appropriate vocabulary, or at least for alternative words when articulating religious devotion, has spread to Sunday mornings around the world, and I speak and sing words to and about God in regular assembly worship that were wholly untried even in my grandparents' generation.

Of course, as periodically has happened in the past, some church authorities have been so confident in only their own way to chart the creedal path that ignorance and cruelty of many kinds have resulted. And yes, over the last several centuries, minimally educated readers of the complex text of the Bible, newly available and affordable in their own vernacular, meant that much ill-informed textual interpretation of the Scriptures has been passed around and accepted. Surely at least some of Rome's theologians in the fifteenth century objected to lay access to the Bible for precisely this reason, that without appropriate education and authorized training, Christian doctrine could go sailing off the edge of the earth into the wild blue yonder. ***Question:*** *Has it?*

From John Updike, in "Seven Stanzas at Easter," in the twentieth century:

Make no mistake: if He rose at all
it was as His Body:
if the cells' dissolution did not reverse,
the molecules reknit,
the amino acids rekindle, the Church
will fall. . . .
Let us not mock God with metaphor,
analogy, sidestepping,
transcendence. . . .
And if we have an angel at the tomb,
make it a real angel,
weighty with Max Planck's quanta,
vivid with hair. . .[2]

Yet the scientific revolution, by asserting that truth is achieved only via facts proved by experimentation, has hoped to maintain its own academic procedures over against any and all linguistic experimentation, and so has convinced many Christians to choose facts as the sole way to travel toward truth.[3] In the fourth century, Ambrose preached that the star that led the magi to God was Christ.[4] But in recent centuries, Christians have searched historic star charts to determine the facts behind such an extraordinary star.[5] Indeed, a reliance on facts has been a religious comfort to many Christians who are understandably upset by a century of critical biblical scholarship that casts doubt on the historicity of much in the Bible. ***Question:*** *Was there a star over Bethlehem, or wasn't there a star? What is a star?*

Especially when invoking and describing the Trinity, believers can find themselves swimming alongside the ark of the church, rather than assembling on its deck for prayer. For centuries, theologians, preachers, and hymnwriters have presented language that tries to describe the Trinity accurately, or, conversely, to celebrate its ineffable mystery. Some have attempted both. But it may be that the difficulty the baptized face when speaking to and of the triune God is one of the reasons that after the Enlightenment, deism rose to replace the church's commitment to salvation through the Trinity. Even now, not everyone who, as a Christian, writes about God begins and concludes all things with the mystery of the Trinity.[6]

Figures of Speech and God

Notwithstanding the value of factual speech, when speaking to and about God, literal wording must stretch. Even when we strive

> *From Gertrude of Helfta in the thirteenth century:*
>
> In order to refer to things familiar to this lower world and to come down to the level of human weakness, Holy Scripture describes things by means of visible forms, and thus impresses on our imagination spiritual ideas by means of beautiful images which excite our desires. Thus they speak now of a land flowing with milk and honey, now of flowers and of perfumes. Read the Apocalypse of St. John and you will find Jerusalem ornamented with gold and silver and pearls and other kinds of gems. Now we know that there is nothing of this sort in heaven where, however, nothing is lacking. But if none of these things is to be found there materially, all are there spiritually.[7]

for accuracy, when we imagine that our theology and our prayer convey a clear meaning, we come to realize that if the sounds we make are directed toward God, the words will get altered in some way. One scholar of religious language, Ian Ramsey, used the categories of "model" and "qualifier" to indicate that human words could only attempt to speak accurately of God.[8] A secondary word must qualify the primary noun in some way. If *judge* is the noun applied to God, *merciful* changes the picture. Dictionaries attempt to indicate the accepted literal meanings of a word, thus providing the edges of our shared communication, but when dealing with religious faith and devotion, since God goes beyond human thought and expression, our sentences must go beyond, must make unlikely comparisons, must both convey personal emotion and cultivate communal meaning.

We Christians attempt to tell the truth, to compose prayers and hymns with sentences open enough to receive God, and yet we cannot rely on factual speech to accomplish this goal. Our words must move beyond literal description, since God, being God, cannot be seen or heard or touched in the same way that humans can see and hear and touch the things of the created order. When believers testify to having seen or heard or touched God, they must employ "figures of speech," and it is these figures of speech about the Trinity that are the topic of this book. ***Question:*** *Since we know that scientifically there is no "up," what in the world do we Christians mean when we say that God is up?*

That the God worshiped by Christians cannot be fully known by factual speech is typified by the biblical tradition of the name of God. "God" is a common noun, capitalized only at the beginning of English sentences or when monotheistic believers designate the sole true deity whom they worship. But what about God's name? Justin Martyr wrote in the second century, "No one can utter the name of the ineffable God: and anyone who dares to say that there is a name raves with a hopeless madness."[9] ***Question:*** *Are some theologians raving mad?*

Yet there is an impressive collection of devout and scholarly studies affirming one term or another as God's true name, each of the options relying to some degree or becoming entangled with a prior figure of speech. In the twentieth century, some Christian theologians have asserted that the triune God does have a literal name—Father, Son, and Holy Spirit—which comes from and illumines our baptismal faith, and Christians must employ that name for acceptable worship.[10] The conflicted question of alternatives for "Father, Son, and Spirit" will be dealt with in chapter 6. But here we can quickly trace the trajectory of what some Christians affirm as God's literal name—the tetragrammaton—which was then abbreviated for the purpose of reverence, and later evolved into a substitute, a cultural figure of speech—Lord—a human title for the divine.

In the Hebrew Bible, God's name is usually notated as the tetragrammaton, those four consonants without vowels, rendered in most

Christian contemporary biblical translations as LORD.[11] Because in English the cultural use of the word *lord* has a male meaning far more readily accessible than is the complicated linguistic history of rendering the Hebrew name of the biblical God, Christians in recent decades have searched for an alternate solution to the rendering of YHWH. The suggestion to spell out the consonants with vowels, as in "Yahweh," has been widely rejected, as constituting offense to Jews. Also, while some Jews claim that the name represents deep breathing, its alien sound diminishes its popularity as a term of direct address for contemporary English-speaking Christians.[12]

This search is especially complicated given the theological tradition that in English a homonym for LORD, *lord*, meaning "master," has been a standard way to designate Jesus of Nazareth. English translations of Mary Magdalene's encounter with the risen Christ have capitalized on this homonym, rendering *kyrios* in John 20:15 as "sir" and three verses later as "Lord," and thus narrating Mary's newfound faith in the resurrection. But because of this historic practice, given that Christianity is a translation religion, the mystery of the divine name has been reshaped by the male image of "master," a commonplace noun serving as the figure of speech for the divine.[13] Furthermore, the Nicene creed names the Third Person of the Trinity as Lord. Thus, in the English language, LORD/Lord has become a

> *From John of Damascus in the eighth century:*
>
> For we see images in created things intimating to us dimly reflections of the divine; as when we say that there is an image of the holy Trinity, which is beyond any beginning, in the sun, its light and its ray, or in a fountain welling up and the stream flowing out and the flood, or in our intellect and reason and spirit, or a rose, its flower and its fragrance.[14]

fundamental linguistic statement of Trinitarian belief. If we are looking at a printed text, the distinction between LORD and Lord is clear, but much of communal worship is heard, not read, and it is not clear what is in the mind of worshipers when addressing "Lord." Thus, each of the following chapters will contribute something to this LORD/Lord discussion. ***Question:*** *Do you know of and advocate any Christian alternative to the continued oral use of LORD/Lord for the Trinity?*

Despite much desire for literal descriptions of God, Christians encounter in the Bible and in Christian tradition a plethora of figures of speech for the divine. Some of these figures are objective: God is a rock. Some are anthropomorphic: God is a king. Some figures are traditional, as when the biblical authors write, perhaps unconsciously, of God as a "he." Some are innovative: is it appropriate and helpful to speak of God as a child?[15] Some of these figures of speech constitute the primary vocabulary of baptized Christians: God as Father. Other figures of speech are rooted in personal poetic reflection—for example, God as Ringmaster[16]—which may or may not be accessible or even acceptable in communal worship. Some are based in historic memories: God leading the armies into battle. Others rely on ancient mythic tales to carry divine mercy: God is praised for slaying the sea monster. ***Question:*** *What do you think about God being invoked as our Ground of Being?*

God via Similes

The most obvious and direct figure of speech practiced by Christians when speaking to and about God is simile. Simile is genuinely a factual expression: when asserting that God is like the sun, the statement is meant to be heard literally. In some way, God, whom we cannot see, actually resembles the sun, which we can. Perhaps of all the figures of speech it is simile that most satisfies literalists, since its minimal claims are meant to be heard as truthful.[17]

The author of the biblical book of Hosea was masterful at simile. If we are accustomed to an ancient God conquering in battle, the author of Hosea says, "I will not save them by bow, or by sword" (Hos 1:7). Rather, it is like the phenomena and creatures of nature that God will act. "I will pour out my wrath like water" (5:10). The appearance of the LORD "is as sure as the dawn," who "will come to us like the showers, like the spring rains that water the earth" (6:3). The author likens God also to wild animals: "I will become like a lion to them, like a leopard, like a bear robbed of her cubs . . . I will devour them as a wild animal would mangle them" (13:7–8). Perhaps most shocking comes the simile in Hosea 5:12: "I am like maggots to Ephraim." Yet God promises forgiveness in Hosea 14:8: "I am like an evergreen cypress," plants that remain green throughout the year. The author is creatively searching through nature, locating rain, trees, and animals that are in some way like God. Only occasionally does the author of Hosea invoke a simile with which we are familiar: in their past, God was "to them like those who lift infants to their cheeks" (11:4). Chapter by chapter, accessible similes, mostly from nature, propose to the people ways to imagine a God of both justice and mercy. ***Question:*** ***How is God like a maggot?***

God via Metaphors

> *From Denise Levertov's "Flickering Mind," in the twentieth century:*
>
> Lord, not you,
> it is I who am absent. . . .
> You are the stream, the fish, the light,
> the pulsing shadow,
> you the unchanging presence, in whom all moves and changes.[18]

The most significant seminal study of metaphor arising in the twentieth century was the work of Paul Ricoeur, who described how metaphor makes us see two things at once, producing a clash of meanings and a breaking of old categories.[19] Some recent biblical studies have focused on the role of metaphor in religious language.[20] Yet there are of course scholars who deny that biblical references to, for example, God's "mighty hand and outstretched arm" are metaphors.[21] For these Christians, biblical speech is necessarily more literal than metaphorical, and one's faith is called to embrace the incongruity of such a divinity. Yet the Bible and the Christian tradition are replete with metaphors, and in liturgical language, the metaphors pile onto one another, mixing without restraint.[22] Metaphors are surprising, sometimes shocking. Metaphors assert an untruth; they speak nonliterally. In metaphors, A equals B, and yet we know that A indeed does not equal B. Despite what we sing on Sunday morning, we know that God is not a rock. Metaphors superimpose what cannot genuinely fit together, and so the believers must move things around in their minds in order to find a place for the truth hidden in the falsity. A metaphor talks about two different things at the same time, producing a tension between the two meanings. Part of our bewilderment arises since it is not only that A is illumined by B: rather, A has been altered by B. Metaphor needs to take its time to effect such transformation. The religious texts must come at us slowly, so that the succinct nature of the metaphor is not lost among the many extra kindly syllables that similes provide.

The Gospel according to John is a thesaurus of metaphors. Perhaps the emerging church needed all those decades between the life of Jesus and the composition of the Johannine Gospel for such a metaphoric imagination to develop and for such disconcerting claims to be welcomed. In John, Jesus of Nazareth is the Logos (1:14): was this Hellenistic imagery that we find in the prologue already a feature of Jewish discourse, or do we credit the fourth evangelist with this metaphor?[23] Repeatedly in the fourth Gospel, Jesus is asked a literal question, to which he responds with a metaphor.[24] In, with, and under the stories of resurrection faith, the author refers to who and what Jesus is by calling him Son of God (1:34), yet this is a God who in the tradition can have no literal son, only a father-like relationship with the king (Ps 2:7). In John, Jesus is also the lamb (1:29), rabbi (1:38), Messiah (1:41), king of Israel (1:49), Son of Man (1:51), temple (2:21), bridegroom (3:29), water (4:14), the prophet (6:14), bread (6:35), the Holy One (6:69), light of the world (9:5), gatekeeper (10:3), gate (10:7), good shepherd (10:11), the resurrection (11:25), teacher and lord (13:13), the way and truth and life (14:6), vine (15:1), friend (15:14). The fourth Gospel presents this astonishing array of metaphors as replacement for a literal and factual description of an executed itinerant preacher. Many of these metaphors will be explored more fully in chapter 4, figures of speech that the fourth evangelist recognized as beyond the grasp of Jesus's disciples. ***Question:*** *How ought we make best sense of the metaphor of Christ as the Son of Man?*

Often in the psalms the metaphor is lodged in the verb, which for reasons of space will not be dealt with in this book. But, briefly here, in Psalm 37:13, the LORD laughs. In Psalm 147, God is assigned over twenty different verbs. In Psalm 104, God is lauded for stretching out the heavens (v. 2), riding on the wings of the wind (3), covering the earth with the seas (6), thundering (7), setting a boundary (9), making springs gush forth (10), giving drink to animals (11), watering the mountains (13), causing grass to grow (14), making the moon to mark the seasons (19), making darkness (20), taking away breath (29), sending forth the spirit (30), renewing the face of the earth (30), yet also touching the mountains and they smoke (32). These verbs employ anthropomorphism; that is, the words borrow human activities to describe divine actions. Such anthropomorphisms turn God momentarily—and erroneously—into a magnified human, formulating a deity who is both totally other and like humankind, a benevolent Zeus in the sky. ***Question:*** *What is beneficial and what is destructive to Christian faith when Zeus functions as a framework for our God?*

God via Epithets

An epithet is a term used as a descriptive substitution for the name or title of a person. To call one's spouse Sweetheart is to employ an epithet. The shorthand that characterizes an epithet proposes a term that is partial, inadequate to the whole. To rely on an epithet for God might seriously diminish the amount of information conveyed, and yet divine epithets are common in Christian speech. Such epithets may be descriptors such as Deliverer or abstractions such as Strength. An epithet that has recently received considerable attention is Wisdom.

Reminiscent of the anthropomorphism of an Ancient Near Eastern goddess, Hokmah/Sophia/Wisdom came into Christian use as a designation of Christ. ***Question:*** *To which Persons of the Trinity does the epithet Wisdom direct your thoughts?*

Epithets that are nouns rely on the worshipers' knowledge of the substitution to imbue the expression with value. For example, to employ the epithet Redeemer for God appropriately, one must have in mind the worldview in which a person owned other persons, holding them in servitude; for their freedom, someone must redeem, that is, pay their cost, to the current owner. The medieval believer was taught that the current owner from whom God redeemed the sinner was the devil, who had acquired humans as a result of the Fall. ***Question:*** *What meanings do twenty-first-century Christians give to the biblically important but currently archaic epithet Redeemer?*

> *From Charles Causley, "I am the Great Sun," in the twentieth century:*
>
> I am the great sun, but you do not see me,
> I am your husband, but you turn away. . .
> I am the captain but you do not obey. . .
> I am the city where you will not stay. . .[25]

God via Parables

The succinct brilliance of parables has assisted in their being literalized, preachers turning some of them into indelible narratives in Christian consciousness. The metaphoric surprise conveyed by those New Testament parables that scholars judge to be most authentic to Jesus's ministry has in many cases been whited out. That God resembles a shepherd has lost its several first-century connotations: that an ideal head of state is likened to a shepherd, or that a real-life shepherd is lower class, a rural and ritually unclean worker. Preachers are faced with the task of altering a commonplace, sentimental, and wholly unrealistic depiction of a shepherd into the God-human who altered all of history. That God is likened to a woman who sweeps her house to find a lost coin has often been laid aside by an androcentric worldview. Yet in these two parables (Luke 15:1–10), it is not God who participates in the action, but "heaven," with "the angels in heaven" rejoicing in the repentance of the sinner. ***Question:*** *How often have you encountered a depiction of God as a woman sweeping her house?*

In Matthew 13:34, the evangelist writes, "Jesus told the crowds all these things in parables; without a parable he told them nothing." What Matthew calls parables include what literary scholars would term allegories: lengthy stories with many parallels to an exterior meaning, rather than pithy metaphoric sayings. These detailed parables have had enduring power in Christian imagination as depictions of God. Some are sustained yet benign figures of speech—for example the "landowner" who pays all employees identically, no matter how long their service (Matt 20:1–16). Yet others of these parables are troublesome: a "king" tortures a slave who was heartless to a colleague (Matt 18:23–35); a "king" ejects a guest who was not attired properly (Matt 22:1–14). Especially the parable of the final judgment (Matt 25:31–46) has consistently been literalized in Christian catechesis, terrifying some of the faithful. ***Question:*** *Are the goats ever forgiven?*

God via Narratives

In many of the biblical narratives of historical fact or religious faith, God functions as a character in the story. Perhaps because narrative is so memorable, perhaps even when trying to imagine the transcendent

God, believers welcome a story that can carry the faith, and so the scriptural narratives that include God as a participant in the story weigh mightily in Christian imagination. That many children's stories and religious legends anthropomorphize animals indicates the perhaps universal reliance on this literary technique to foster the hearer's sympathy. We can only hope that the biblical narratives can lead us into the inexpressible mystery of God, rather than merely replacing wonder at the inconceivable God with pleasure at a Superman tale.

A well-known example of God being anthropomorphized in a biblical narrative is God taking an evening walk in the garden of Eden (Gen 3:8). Given our scientific worldview, it may well be that this literal anthropomorphizing of God in the Genesis creation stories has worked against contemporary religious belief. Sometimes the scriptural text is more oblique. For example, Jacob is maimed by a wrestler who subsequently is identified, more or less, as God (Gen 34:24–30). One anthropomorphized biblical narrative that has become treasured in the history of Christian art is the story of the three visitors to Abraham and Sarah. The Hebrew text interchanges references to "three men" and "lord," which has led Christians, although not the authors of the Hebrew text, to see the Trinity at the table (Gen 18:1–8). Sometimes God functions in the narrative apart from any anthropomorphism, as when Elijah encounters God as "a sound of sheer silence" (1 Kgs 19:12); yet even in this narrative, God speaks, using human language (1 Kgs 19:15). ***Question:*** *Is harm done when children's Bible story books depict God as a male?*

Perhaps the practice undertaken by many biblical authors to utilize angels in narratives was a perceptive way to describe God meeting with and conversing with humans. In some narratives, for example, the account of the saving of Hagar (Gen 16:7–13), angels and God take turns interacting with humans. It may be that the testimony of divine contact with humans finds angels a necessary storytelling technique.[26] Yet, as the author of Hebrews writes, it is not angels that God calls Son (Heb 1:5). For it may be that the Christian mystery of the incarnation welcomes the practice of anthropomorphism, despite its obvious dangers for monotheistic belief. In Jesus Christ, God becomes human while remaining divine, not merely in figures of speech, but in both the historical memories about a first-century itinerant faith healer and in centuries of the baptismal creed. ***Question:*** *Should Christian prayers make more mention of angels than recent texts are wont to do?*

God via Anthropomorphisms

> *From James E. Griffiss in the twentieth century:*
>
> The human tendency is often to lose a sense of the mystery of God by our domestication of the divine.[27]

We come now to those anthropomorphic figures of speech that are paramount in Christian text and consideration: God as male in gender, God as father and son, God as person.

Brought into Christian controversy during the early decades of the feminist movement was the relentless problem of the tradition of divine gender. Even in the fifth century, this issue was discussed, when for example Gregory of Nazianzus taunted those who imagined that because the nouns used in naming God bore a specific linguistic gender, that gender applied also to God, who has no sex.[28] Given the immense scholarly attention paid over the last five decades to the question of divine gender and the consequent controversy arising among worshiping Christians and addressed by ecclesiastic leadership, here is merely a recent update to this issue.[29]

It has been the case that in Christianity divine gender has functioned not only as a figure of speech, noted explicitly as such by the theologians who crafted the Nicene creed, but also as perhaps the most determinative "image of God" granted to humans.[30] That God is spoken of as male has brought Zeus into our churches and our piety, and since as Karl Marx has taught us, power is never given up voluntarily, there has been considerable resistance to lessening or deleting the sometimes hidden androcentrism of male pronouns. Furthermore, Christian theologians have not come to any agreement about how essential for doctrine and faithful discipleship is the divine masculine. In addition, translating the Scriptures without use of the divine male pronoun is exceedingly difficult, and many preachers find too tedious the task of deleting the masculine pronouns from their speech.

But there is more. The historic understanding in the West that humans were divided between two genders and the practice in many cultures that each of the two has a distinct and defined role in society has been challenged by a new sense that gender is fluid, a self-chosen category for one's individual

From Jacque B. Jones, "We Long to Know Her," in the twenty-first century:

We long to hear her, bold thunder
of heaven,
voice among voices that summon
the soul;
without her presence, there is
no completeness,
with her unheard, heaven cannot
be whole.
We know her laughter is piercing
the cosmos;
we know she judges injustice on earth.
Shelter and shield of the hopeless
and helpless,
from her we learn of our infinite worth.[31]

life. Historic religious reliance on God's role in determining and maintaining essentialist gender has given way to an openness about the human body and the malleable inclination of the individual psyche. The question whether liturgical texts should minimize biblical male pronouns for God, or indeed wholly eliminate this convention, now must also ask what in American society "he" or "she" mean. Because of the tradition that "he" in English sometimes, in some centuries, has nongendered usage, authorizing the use of "she" for God does not solve the gender problem: it may indeed actually heighten the issue of the importance of gender as a figure of speech. Later chapters will address this question in more detail. ***Question:*** *Ought God to be imagined as androgynous?*

Recent theological discussion has witnessed considerable debates about the contemporary meaning of the biblical and historical reliance on the naming of God as Father and Son. The linguistic parameters of this book classify Father and Son as premier examples of Christian figures of speech. The Bible and theology are employing figures of speech when speaking as if God is in some way like a male and that God's being toward Jesus is in some way like the relationship between a father and a son. Some theologians have stressed that the incarnation made this language not only appropriate but required in Christianity. Yet the paganism of first-century Rome made commonplace the language of a divine

> *From Emily Dickinson in the nineteenth century:*
>
> Who were "the Father and the Son"
> We pondered when a child,
> And what had they to do with us
> And when portentous told . . . .
> We blush, that Heaven if we achieve—
> Event ineffable—
> We shall have shunned until ashamed
> To own the Miracle—[32]

Father and Son: Hercules was the son of the god Jupiter and the mortal Alcmena, and the first official act of the emperor Nero was to deify his adoptive father Claudius, which resulted in Nero's being lauded as "the son of [the] god." Thus, it is inaccurate to suggest that this language is uniquely sacred speech of the baptized. There is currently no consensus in the churches as to how faithfully Christians can speak of God without recourse to the figures of speech Father and Son. We shall look at this question in detail as we list dozens of innovative figures of speech that embellish or replace classic terminology. ***Question:*** *How are we to evaluate the recent use of the metaphor "Mother" for God?*

In the explication of the Trinity, the fifth century saw theological acceptance of the Greek label *hypostasis* and the Latin term *persona* as linguistically necessary in delineating the mystery of the Three-in-One. Some recent theologians have sought alternatives to the English term "person": Karl Barth wrote of "modes of being," and Karl Rahner of "modes of subsistence." Yet the category "person" remains standard Christian speech.[33] Yet as applied to God, "person" is itself a figure of speech. In our society, its overwhelming usage is referring to a single center of personality and is a complimentary way to designate the human. Thus, its adoption by Christian theologians can be thought of as supreme metaphor, a figure of speech so pervasive as to minimize reflective thought. I hope that my capitalizing the word *Person* helps to indicate that the word in Trinitarian context means something other than its common usage. But I mean to indicate that even the theological term *Person* is a figure of speech, and although the best that we have yet found, a term that masks the mystery of the divine. ***Question:*** *Is it helpful for you to think of God as either Person, a Person, or Persons?*

Figures of Speech in the Twenty-First Century

For those of us who treasure the habit of accumulating figures of speech for God, we find much in the twenty-first century that supports our endeavor. Here we can briefly consider critical biblical studies, the feminist movements, the use of the three-year lectionary, the weekly praying of psalms, the claims of postmodernism, the proposals of cognitive linguistics, and even the entertainment industry as roads that lead to a ready acceptance of metaphoric communication.

Biblical scholars, some of whom are practicing Christians, have published studies that boldly go where many clergy fear to go, in tracing mythic and metaphoric foundations of narratives and images in the Bible.[34] Thus what might appear to be factual narratives about historical persons and situations are actually imaginative stories of faith inspired by prior religious and cultural tales. In such biblical accounts, the details receive their fullest meaning when the figure of speech is probed. The gold, frankincense, and myrrh of the magi in Matthew 2:1 make no sense as literal gifts to a genuine infant. Rather, they indicate that Matthew's tradition acclaimed Jesus as the king (gold) who in light of his coming death (myrrh) was to be worshipped as a god (frankincense). It is only when these details are recognized as figures of speech that the narrative of the visit of the magi is intelligible. Furthermore, the scriptural habit of what scholars now term "intertextuality" relies on quotations from one part of the Bible used metaphorically in another. In John 6, the fourth evangelist stresses that our understanding the narratives in which Jesus feeds the multitudes relies on our knowing the ancient tales of the manna. The twentieth century witnessed a surge of scholarly interest in the biblical technique of metaphor, with the innovative claim that without understanding metaphor, we miss the primary meaning of the text.[35] ***Question:*** *What do we definitively know about the actual human Jesus of Nazareth?*

The widespread adoption of the ecumenical three-year lectionary and its parent the Roman lectionary hold before all worshipers the distinctive character of each of the four Gospels. In the second century Irenaeus argued against a single summary text constructed out of the four Gospels.[36] The church, he claimed, needed all four accounts because they were different, and the three-year lectionary makes these differences more evident than did the one-year medieval lectionary, or indeed, does any lectionary that pulls the Sunday readings without reference to their source from any of the four biblical writings. By recognizing that the four passion accounts are not accurate factual records of the event, believers can benefit from the fourfold imagery of Christ as hidden messiah in Mark, fulfiller of promise in Matthew, master of forgiveness in Luke, and incarnate God in John. The differences between the passion accounts in the four Gospels are carried by the many figures of speech upon which they rely. For example, only in John 18 do the soldiers who are arresting Jesus fall to the ground before him. ***Question:*** *What would the author of Mark's Gospel say about Luke's ascension narrative?*

Furthermore, the three-year lectionary has offered to countless assemblies the practice of singing a psalm each week as a complement to the readings.[37] These psalms give to the worshiping assembly a regular adventure in biblical figures of speech, and they train the faithful in the practice of metaphor as a welcome aspect of the language of faith.[38] On Epiphany, the faithful sing from Psalm 72 about kings offering gifts to Israel's king, thus lending some grandeur to the children's pageant about the visit of the magi. On the Sundays of the Baptism of our Lord and on the festival of the Holy Trinity in year B, the lectionary invites us to chant Psalm 29, in which a cosmic divine voice breaks the cedars of Lebanon and strips the forests bare. Here the New Testament accounts of the voice at Jesus's baptism and of Jesus's conversation with Nicodemus are undergirded by the ancient pagan divine power that can destroy the creation itself. The figure of speech in the psalm has transformed how we receive the narrative in the Gospel.

The claims put forward by postmodernist thinkers have been unsettling to many Christians.[39] That there is nothing we can assert as "truth" can be particularly upsetting to believers, many of whom have been taught to trust that the best of their religious tradition does indeed offer them genuine God-given truth. Postmodernism states that if "truth" exists, we have no access to it, since all accounts and perceptions made by humans are limited by their own situation. The literal facticity of the Bible must be replaced with faith in God and companionship of the baptized community, both of which are cultivated in expressions marked by figures of speech. However, given that much in the Scriptures, even some of what is told about Jesus, is disconcerting to contemporary believers, this relativizing of "truth" can actually be a gift to the Christian assembly, since our trust must lie in God, not in a literalized religious text. ***Question:*** *What is one claim about God recorded in the Scriptures that you hope to goodness is not literally true?*

> *From Les Murray, "Poetry and Religion," in the twentieth century:*
>
> Full religion is the large poem flowing
> in repetition. . .
> God is the poetry caught in any religion,
> caught, not imprisoned. . . .[40]

Recently the discipline of linguistics has focused on a cognitive theory of metaphor.[41] According to this mode of thought, the endless process of extending human knowledge means that words we might now assume to be literal were at root metaphoric. Indeed, all language arises in metaphor, the name of one known thing transferred over to an unknown thing, and it is the reality of the human body seeing and speaking that occasions all speech.[42] Despite the historic Western reliance on literalism, this linguistic theory says that there is no such thing as wholly literal language. Some theologians have then argued that cognitive linguistics bridges any supposed gap between the literal and the figurative in classic religious texts. For religious participation, this reliance on metaphor is not a danger to faith but rather the process toward genuine intelligibility. Since each religious metaphor says something of the whole, the explosion in recent decades of hymns filled with multiple figures of speech can be lauded as a product of and direction toward the divine.[43]

Finally, we can reflect here for a moment on the contemporary film industry.[44] When in the eighteenth century authors first began to write novels, they advertised their work as memoirs, as true histories, since the assumption was that only factual material would have appeal to readers. Yet two centuries later, children and countless adults of all ages are loyal adherents of the myths and metaphors of superhero films: the Star Trek tales, the Star Wars series, The Lord of the Rings saga, and the Harry Potter adventures. The immense power of these films welcomes viewers into an alternate reality

From C. S. Lewis in The Lion, the Witch and the Wardrobe, *in the twentieth century:*

"He'll be coming and going. One day you'll see him and another you won't. He doesn't like being tied down—and of course he has other countries to attend to. It's quite all right. He'll often drop in. Only you mustn't press him. He's wild, you know. Not like a *tame* lion."[45]

that has perhaps surprising but intensely meaningful connections to one's current existence. Some of these meanings are spoken aloud, while others are hidden in one's consciousness, but in either case, these metaphors play a substantial role in undergirding personal and communal life. The complaint one often hears from clergy that contemporary people do not "get" metaphor seems to disregard the astonishing effect of these films to attract viewers, lure them into nonliteral worldviews, and form communities of like-minded adherents.

Early in the twentieth century the eminent scholar Rudolf Otto taught us to think about religion as attention to the Wholly Other, the "numinous" marked by *mysterium tremendum*, what is inner and what is beyond being able to reach out to us.[46] But as members of Western society and heirs of centuries of humanism, most of us are better at scanning the daily headlines for the facts of human life than we are at meditating on transcendent divine mystery. It seems that we wish to tolerate only so much openness, only a bit of holiness, lest our very selves get lost in a place that has no boundaries.

Yet as we hope to become "green Christians," to know ourselves as creatures of God's creating, to recognize our limits, to accept the reality of death, to honor ecological concerns, and to dedicate ourselves to the needs of others, it is time to admit that our religious knowledge is indeed incomplete. We are not given some literal facts about God and salvation that we might wish for. Rather, religion is constructed by figures of speech that are handed down to us from a past we no longer trust and are offered to a present assembly we hope to serve within a future that confronts us with endless questions.

It has been the intention of this first chapter to welcome twenty-first century believers into the necessity of religious figures of speech. Of the figures of speech that have been introduced, many of the nouns will be discussed in greater detail in subsequent chapters. Albeit that in religious speech similes are partial, metaphors are falsehoods, epithets require explanation, parables are unsettling, biblical narratives are largely statements of faith, and anthropomorphisms can tempt us to forgo trust in the divine, the fact that much of Christian belief is conveyed through figures of speech is finally good news. For the interpretation of odd similes and of slippery metaphors requires the participation of the whole community. A text marked by figures of speech assumes a community of readers who together recognize its metaphoric intention.[47] Thankfully, in religion, we are not alone. A Christian description of God is not a simple text that I can read all by myself. I need to hear from you, you need to listen to me, we attend to the past, we walk side by side into the future. For believers, upheld by the promises of the Trinity, we hope to greet one another in God with the peace of the risen Christ and the power of the Spirit despite the incompleteness of human speech and the inadequacies of historical records. To our surprise, we can gather each Sunday at an empty tomb, proclaim an ancient name, and unite in singing "Holy, holy, holy."

2

AN EXAMPLE: GOD THE FIRE

IN RECENT DECADES "father" and "mother" have received considerable analysis as to their appropriateness as figures of speech in addressing and referring to the Trinity. Among the dozens of figures that this book will list, many merit lengthy discussions of their origin, meanings, and challenges. Although throughout this book most figures of speech will be dealt with in brief, let this chapter's focus on God the Fire exemplify the depth with which we could contemplate many other figures of speech for God. Our concluding question will be whether in the twenty-first century fire ought to be invoked more often than it currently is when praying to and describing God.

Fire for Humankind

While some of the ancients considered fire to be one of the four constituent elements of the earth, Christians believe that because God created the universe, in regular, hidden, and sometimes surprising ways, all the created earth carries the mark of the Creator. Given this mark of grace on all the natural world, the Christian assembly can rely on many items of the earth to carry divine power to the community. Water, bread, and wine are the primary earthly vehicles that carry the church into the encounter with God, but in a lesser way also fire can bespeak God to the people.

For fire to be kindled in the center of our circle of worshipers and to illumine our occasions of prayer, we need first to contain its natural ferocity for our purposes. About a million years ago, homo erectus tamed fire. Archaeological investigation of the Wonderwerk Cave in Northern Cape Province, South Africa, suggests that the fire-taming may have taken place perhaps more like one and a half million years ago.[1] By taming fire, our forebears could bring light into the darkness, warm themselves in the cold, protect themselves from predators, and cook their food, thereby consuming more calories and over the eons enlarging their brain capacity. The people could gather around such a controlled fire and so become a community. Thanks to tamed fire, groups could emigrate from Africa to colder climates and so spread the species around the globe. It is safe to say that without a tamed fire, there would have been no homo sapiens. Yet if humans require fire that is tame, in some ways the earth requires fire that is wild, for even natural forest fires are necessary for some varieties of plants to release their seeds.

Despite the common English expression "the taming of fire," fire is not actually tamed. In our century we stand mute before the wildfires that consume brush and forest, crop fields and human habitations, the power of their conflagrations far beyond that of the firefighters who are killing themselves to extinguish the flames. Wildfires are worsening as Earth's climate changes. Where people could reside, they must now flee, for fire cannot be as controlled as we might wish. Ancient Greek myths imagined that Zeus wanted this power for

From Grace Nichols, "Caribbean Woman Prayer," in the twentieth century:

God de Fadder
God de Mudder
God de Sister
God de Brudder
God de Holy Fire[2]

himself alone and thus punished Prometheus for giving humans fire. It ought not be surprising that some religions have found fire an apt image for ineffable divinity, for fire can symbolize both a peaceful and welcome benevolence granted to human habitation and the virulent and inscrutable might of the universe. ***Question:*** *What has been your experience with the uncontrollable terror of fire?*

Fire in the Bible

Historically prior to the stories that fill the Hebrew Scriptures, the religions of the Ancient Near East employed the imagery of fire. The biblical Psalm 29 has been identified as a close variant of a Canaanite Ugaritic hymn to Baal that was later adapted as a worship resource by the Israelites: "The voice of the LORD flashes forth flames of fire" (Ps 29:7). In Psalm 104, which resembles the Egyptian praise of the sun god Aton, fire and flame are said to be God's ministers. Indeed, the rhetoric of much of the entire Bible is aflame. Sometimes the reference to fire is no more than the author's impressive comparison for the topic at hand. Here are similes: anger "blazes like a flaming fire" (Hos 7:6), and your lust for riches "will eat your flesh like fire" (Jas 5: 3). We encounter also metaphors: "the tongue is a fire" (Jas 3:6). By treating with kindness those who have harmed you, you "heap burning coals on their heads" (Rom 12:20). The words of John the Baptist in Matthew and in Luke, that the coming one "will baptize you with the Holy Spirit and fire" (Matt 3:11), and of Jesus in Luke, "I came to bring fire to the earth" (Luke 12:49), are intended to be interpreted figuratively, an extreme literary comparison made in order to indicate the shocking purpose of Jesus's confrontation with evil.

In many places throughout the Bible, God's very presence is likened to fire or is seen as fire. God's word is "a fire in your mouth" (Jer 5:14). In one of Scriptures' most significant encounters of the human with the divine, God appears to Moses in the burning bush (Exod 3:2–3). That the fire is burning although the bush is not consumed exemplifies religious paradox: God is fire, but not fire as we know it. Standing on holy ground, we are attracted to but not destroyed by God's fire. To the migrant Israelites God gave light at night by means of a pillar of fire (Exod 13:21), and as with the cloud by day, God was present in the created order for the good of the people. God descended on Mount Sinai in fire (Exod 19:18) and rested over the tabernacle each night "having the appearance of fire" (Num 9:16). In Ezekiel's vision, the divine throne is flanked by flame (Ezek 1:13, 27); in Daniel's vision, fire flows from the divine throne (Dan 7:10); and in John's vision, God's eyes are like a flame of fire (Rev 1:14). The four living creatures, which appear as flashes of lightning, surround a bright fire (Ezek 1:13). In heaven is also "a sea of glass mixed with fire" (Rev 15:2), here the seer relying on a mixed metaphor to describe the inexpressible presence of God. ***Question:*** *Can Christians who no longer rely on actual fires in their homes find fire a sign of the presence of a mighty God?*

> *From a sixth century kontakia of Romanos, in which John the Baptist addresses Jesus who is coming to him for baptism:*
>
> "What do you seek from a human, O Lover of mankind? Why do you bow your head beneath my hand? For it is not used to holding fire."[3]

Fire can be a sign of the gift of divine favor. God's covenant with Abram is sealed with a ritual of a fire pot and a flaming torch (Gen 15:17). The burnt offerings that fill the Hebrew Scriptures, from Abel's firstling of his flock (Gen 4:4) to Noah's massive offering "of every clean animal and of every clean bird" (Gen 8:20) to the detailed regulations of Leviticus 1–7 meant to connect the human with the divine by means of fire. It is as if there must be death for life to appear, and in religious sacrifices fire carries the death to the life-giving God. Fire can serve as a means of ritual purification (Num 31:23). In a striking metaphor of mercy, Zechariah receives God's promise to protect Jerusalem with fire: "For I will be a wall of fire all around it" (Zech 2:5). God's fire can indicate divine acceptance, as when God accepts Elijah's offering against the prophets of Baal (1 Kgs 18:38), when David's offering is graced with "fire from heaven" (1 Chron 21:26), and when Solomon's prayer is answered as "fire came down from heaven" (2 Chron 7:1). ***Question:*** *In our time, can the natural power of fire be seen as a sign of divine favor?*

Biblical fire is also a sign of divine punishment. Perhaps these stories indicate an ancient notion that God is copying, if not inspiring, the practice of burning what is evil, thus purging the community of wickedness. The conquered city of Jericho is burned down (Josh 6:24), and persons guilty of some stipulated crimes are to be executed by burning (Lev 20:14). Many passages in both Testaments liken God's displeasure to fire. The prophet writes that God has "consumed them with the fire of my wrath" (Ezek 22:31), and the sons of Aaron, by offering to God what is called "unholy fire," were consumed by it (Lev 10:1–2).[4] Yet child sacrifice by fire is forbidden (Deut 18:10), although King Ahaz was accused of burning his son (2 Kgs 16:3). Most well-known in our society is the tale of God's destruction of Sodom and Gomorrah by raining down fire from heaven (Gen 19:24). Perhaps the memory of a volcanic eruption had been interpreted by the ancient writers as divine punishment and remembered as literal fire descending from God's throne. For some Christians, the "fire and brimstone" of God's anger is still burning throughout the world, and the lifelong task of the believer is to escape that fire, here and in eternity. For others, God's mercy has done much to quench holy flames, and the fire and brimstone of a literal hell has long since been washed away. ***Questions:*** *Should the account in Genesis 19 of the burning of Sodom and Gomorrah be included in the Sunday lectionary?*

> *From Norman Nicholson, "The Burning Bush," in the twentieth century:*
>
> But stinging tongues like John the
> Baptist shout:
> 'That this is metaphor is no way out.
> It's dogma too, or you make God a liar;
> The bush is still a bush and fire is fire.'[5]

Sometimes it seems that authors of our Scriptures intentionally meant to literalize fire. Many of the descriptions of the apocalypse throughout the Bible give first place to fire. In Paul's metaphorical discussion of building for the kingdom, he refers to the coming revelation "with fire" (1 Cor 3:13). Several of the epistles speak of the coming "flaming fire" (2 Thess 1:8), the destruction of the evil world with fire (2 Pet 3:10). The descriptions of hell in the Gospels—"the chaff he will burn with unquenchable fire" (Matt 3:12), "you will be liable to the hell of fire" (Matt 5:22)—have been literalized throughout much Christian preaching. In explicit metaphors, the Scriptures say that God is a devouring fire (Deut 4:24), that "indeed our God is a consuming fire" (Heb 12:29). Yet the narrative of the prophet Elijah states clearly that, despite expectations, God was not in the fire (1 Kgs 19:12). ***Question:*** *When should Christians literalize the language of divine fire?*

Trinitarian Fire

To consider how the Old Testament can be cited in a discussion of Trinitarian imagery, we need to attend to the hermeneutic that was common in the early church. We are familiar with much contemporary theological study, as well as in denominational parlance, that values interest in and respect for the original meaning of the biblical text. Thus especially in academic circles the title "the Hebrew Bible" has been regularized for approximately three-fourths—if one counts the Apocrypha, four-fifths—of the scriptures that are privately studied and publicly proclaimed and interpreted by Christians. But in a newly printed New Revised Standard Version, Updated Edition, a title page prints the more traditional designation, "The Old Testament." For throughout the formative centuries of the faith, these Hebrew and Aramaic scriptures, read for the most part in their Greek translation the Septuagint, were identified by Greek speakers as "the scriptures" for Christians, the "old" proclamation, the earlier covenant, which inaugurated the "new" testimony.[7] Christians saw the promise of a new covenant (Jer 31:31) to be met by the words of Jesus at the last supper, as cited in the synoptic narratives. This Christian adoption of the older testament is clear in 2 Timothy 3:16: "All scripture is inspired by God and is useful for teaching . . . for instruction in righteousness," the reference to "all scripture" of course referring to the Hebrew Scriptures.

> *From Hildegard of Bingen, in her twelfth century* Scivias*:*
>
> As the flame of a fire has three qualities, so there is one God in the three Persons. By the brilliant light understand the Father; by the red power understand the Son; and by the fiery heat understand the Holy Spirit.[6]

Early theologians readily accepted these Hebrew and Aramaic texts as speaking of the God whom they encountered in Christ, and the theophanies described in the Hebrew Bible were baptized as testifying to the Trinity. As Gregory of Nazianzus wrote, "When I say 'God,' I mean Father and Son and Holy Spirit."[8] The early Christian interpreters of the Scriptures believed that the Second Person of the Trinity was present and active from before the beginning of time and throughout human history, revealing the Godhead long before the incarnation of God in Jesus of Nazareth. Thus, according to this hermeneutic, if in the Septuagint God was heard speaking, it was the Second Person who was speaking. Illuminated manuscripts maintained this understanding into medieval times, when the God who is for example creating the world is pictured as a man, meant to be recognized as Christ.[9] This standard practice of the early church has recently been termed "christophanic exegesis."[10] A primary Christian pericope that exemplifies this style of scriptural exegesis is the Lucan story of the appearance to the risen Christ at Emmaus, when such Christophanic interpretation acclaims Christ "in all the scriptures" (Luke 24:27), not only in a few selected and recognizably messianic passages.[11]

Despite the current scholarly assumption that historical and critical biblical analysis is the most appropriate for Christian use, it is helpful when attending to scriptural rhetoric to remember that Christian theology relied on what Jews now call the Tanakh as foundational in developing Trinitarian belief. It can be said that in their Christological interpretation of the Scriptures, early Christian readers turned the Hebrew Bible into the Old Testament by identifying "the Logos-to-be-incarnate" in narratives and poetry throughout the Septuagint. An example of this Christological interpretation of the Hebrew Bible is the currently popular O Antiphons, in which for example the key of David, the sun at winter solstice, and the king of nations are identified as Christ. ***Question:*** *Is the designation "the Old Testament" problematic?*

> *From Catherine of Siena, in the fourteenth century:*
>
> You are nothing but a fire of love.
> By the fire of love you created us. . . .
> O eternal Trinity!
> O fire ever burning,
> fire that never goes out,
> never dims,
> never can be diminished
> even if the whole world takes fire
> from you.[12]

The theologians whom we call the church fathers, from Justin to Gregory of Nyssa, saw fire in the Hebrew Bible as a manifestation of the Trinity. For example, in catechesis, in preaching and in illustrating the narrative of the burning bush, Christians affirmed that Christ was in the fire.[13] In Isaiah 6, when Isaiah sees the fiery altar in his temple vision, "holy" is acclaimed three times, denoting the mystery of the Trinity. In Daniel 3, the three youths are joined in the fiery furnace with Christ.[14] In the narrative of Pentecost, God's presence is seen in the fire of Sinai now dispersed onto the head of each of the faithful (Acts 2:3). According to this hermeneutic, the Hebrew Scriptures of ancient Israelites are like the trunk of an elm tree with two main branches, one of which grew into Judaism after the destruction of the temple and the other of which sourced

> *From Quodvultdeus, the fifth-century bishop of Carthage:*
>
> Our God chose to appear in no other form than fire. Behold in the fire we see three things: the flame, its brilliance and its heat; yet, though there are three, there is one light. They work together, and, although they work without separation, the flame is one thing, the radiance another, and the heat still another.[15]

the Christian church. In this way of thinking, not only are Christians licensed to borrow the Hebrew Scriptures, but for Trinitarian doctrine they are required to do so. ***Question:*** *Can Christians receive Christian faith through Hebrew narratives that did not originally have this intent, without falling into an antisemitic commandeering of the sacred texts of Jews?*

God as Fire in Christian Ritual

Whether or not current Christian catechesis teaches that Christ is seen in the burning bush, we continue to read the works of especially Christian mystics, female and male, who especially during the eleventh through the fifteenth centuries regularly cited fire as a primary figure of speech for the triune God. The mystery of fire operative in both purification and destruction presented a welcome metaphor for the God before whom the mystics poured out their ecstatic utterances. Yet even if mystical reveries are not to our taste, also in our time Christian communal ritual utilizes fire as a sign of God for the baptized. For example, we process with lighted candles around the nave, we place them in an already well-lit sanctuary, and perhaps on Christmas Eve, to call us to the wonder of a holy event, we offer a lighted candle to each worshiper. ***Question:*** *Given the fear not of fire but of lawsuits, do churches still light real candles?*

For many Christians through the ages, fire is one of the most common symbols for the Holy Spirit, and in our Spirit-focused liturgical rituals fire is at least orally present. On Ash Wednesday, we wear on our foreheads the residue of purifying fire, and on Pentecost, wearing red, we pray for the beneficial effect of divine fire in our midst. Christians hang a banner depicting flames over the baptismal font.

Our prayers at Pentecost, baptisms, confirmations, ordinations, and installations are filled with language alight with flames: "kindle in us the fire of your love," the ninth-century Latin prayer attributed to the eminent theologian and writer Rabanus Maurus echoing in our songs and petitions. We dress ourselves and our worship space in fiery red to commemorate the saints. ***Question:*** *Do you judge the depictions of fire in our liturgical art as both frightening and welcoming, or merely as inconsequential?*

> *From Gertrude of Helfta, in the thirteenth century:*
>
> O devastating coal, my God, burning inextinguishably with living heat, O truly consuming fire, O fiery furnace of ever-increasing heat, from you alone and not otherwise can we receive the power to be reformed to the image and likeness of our original state.[16]

The primary use for Christians of fire is at the Easter Vigil. The common use of the term "vigil" is somewhat misleading, especially given the interpretation that its initial call "The Light of Christ" is the announcement of the resurrection. Perhaps we might refer to this first eucharist of Easter as the Fire Ceremony of the Resurrection. In some assemblies, the presider formally lights the fire, perhaps by striking a flint, thus recalling the centuries in which the tribal shaman renewed the fires of the community at the time of the spring equinox. In other assemblies, a substantial bonfire has been lit without ceremony, and its warmth and the mystery of its flickering invite the assembly to gather around and begin the Easter celebration.

The Vigil proceeds as the paschal candle is lit and leads the assembly into the place of the readings. This little flame of fire we acclaim as the light of Christ, dispelling the darkness of our hearts and minds, in this annual metaphor of the resurrection. We follow the fire into the place of the readings as if we are the ancient Israelites following the pillar of fire through the wilderness, as if we are led by the mystery of the fire of the risen Christ into our future. In the Easter Proclamation, we sing to the candle, praising "the glories of this pillar of fire." We face the candle and find ourselves bonded with believers in the fifth century, when this song of praise was written, as in the words of the Exultet we pray that the risen Christ, embodied in the flame of the candle, will "vanquish the darkness of night."[17] At the conclusion of the Exultet, the fire of the candle becomes Christ the Morning Star, promising life to the whole darkened world. In some traditions, the many Vigil readings taken from the Old Testament culminate with Daniel 3:1–29, the engaging tale of the three faithful youths thrown into the furnace of blazing fire. This story finds its Christian interpretation at Easter: the fourth figure, joining the three in the fire, is an image of the risen Christ, standing with us in each fire of our lives. ***Question:*** *How fully does your assembly celebrate the resurrection through rituals and stories of fire?*

From D. Elton Trueblood, "God, Whose Purpose Is to Kindle," in the twentieth century:

God, whose purpose is to kindle,
now ignite us with your fire.
While the earth awaits your burning,
with your passion us inspire.
Overcome our sinful calmness, stir us
with your saving name.
Baptize with your fiery Spirit, crown
our lives with tongues of flame.[18]

One final consideration: It may be that in keeping with Exodus 20:5–6, which proclaims God's punishments to the third and fourth generations but God's steadfast love to the thousands that follow, Christians rightly praise divine mercy as exceeding divine justice. The several versions of the ecumenical three-year lectionary were designed and promoted by Christians who believe that God's gift of loving purification far exceeds God's decision to burn us at the stake.

There is considerably more in the lectionary of forgiveness than of punishment, and even when divine wrath is heard in the readings, the communal sharing of the gift of bread and wine works to counter the threat. It is almost as if the ancient understanding that God will destroy us with fire is a religion that we have outgrown and that God as Fire is no longer a helpful figure of speech. Certainly, a similar claim is made by some Christians concerning the figure of speech of God as father, that given its support of patriarchy, it ought to be shelved in some library of liturgical antiquities. Yet it may be that by extinguishing all the fire of God from our rhetoric, we have produced a nursery-school edition of the faith, one not mature enough to support us throughout the terrors of living. ***Question:*** *Does your lectionary contain the right balance between God's justice and God's mercy?*

We have considered first fire in the human community, which requires God's gift of fire for wholesome living, and then, assisted by critical studies, fire in the Bible, both God's benedictions and God's punishments described as fire. The Christian tradition has literalized especially some of the most negative of these references. For some Christians, God the Fire evokes a mere can of Sterno, a God too tame, too controlled, a primitive power made unnecessary by electricity. For others, God the Fire suggests too much violence, medieval men burning witches at the stake, contemporary natural wildfires wrecking massive destruction of human habitations. Yet green Christians may find the earthly imagery appropriate, and contemporary Christian art and ritual are keeping alive the metaphor of divine fire, primarily at the revival of the Easter Vigil. Evocation of fire can be a gift to contemporary Christians, since it is a nongendered and nonbinary figure of speech. Our faith is that God is that phenomenon without which human community could not survive; God is the mysterious other that draws all people to attention and awe; God is the purification of all things, preparing what is worthy; God is the destruction of all we view as evil. Perhaps God the Fire can indeed manifest the mystery.

So one more ***question:*** *Is fire a divine figure of speech significant enough for Christians to merit a full chapter in this book?*

3

THE FIRST PERSON, FIGURATIVELY SPEAKING

Who is "God"?

THIS CHAPTER LOOKS through a lengthy list of figures of speech for God. For many entries in this chapter, the word "God" may have been intended to refer to the entire Godhead, while for some Christians, thinking always on the eternal Trinity, the figures of speech listed in this chapter may have referred to the First Person of the Trinity. Those expressions that list three separate names or qualities for the deity will be discussed in chapter 6, with its focus on the Trinity.

To encourage our study of the complexities of imagery for God, we look first at Psalm 60:8, "On Edom I hurl my shoe." In this psalm, written by an ancient anonymous poet, the "I," the speaker of this line, is identified as God. In the parlance of the Ancient Near East, to "throw one's shoe" was to symbolize ownership by laying one's feet onto the property of the vanquished. Edom was an enemy of ancient Israel, and in this psalm the people are begging God to demonstrate authority by conquering Israel's enemy. Thus in this short sentence we encounter a verbal reference to an odd social gesture that is outside our experience, a God who wears shoes and who throws things, a God who promised to dispossess the native peoples in favor of preferred immigrants and invaders, and a God who can be trusted to defeat a national enemy. We might rightly ask, Is this our God? Fortunately, many biblical figures of speech pose fewer challenges for us than does this line from Psalm 60:8, and some are too distant to have much religious meaning for us. ***Question:*** *If you ever pray Psalm 60, what does it mean to you?*

The church's oldest sourcebook of figures of speech for worship is the Book of Psalms, which functioned as the church's earliest hymnal. Thanks to the widespread use of the Roman Catholic Lectionary for Mass and the ecumenical Revised Common Lectionary with their appointed responsory psalms, worshiping assemblies are newly becoming accustomed to many unfamiliar biblical figures of speech for God.[1] Not all 150 psalms are appointed for use in the three-year lectionaries, and we here begin by looking at both the objective and the anthropomorphic figures of speech in a psalm that is not assigned in these lectionaries. This list of figures of speech is amplified by reference to the three sources that I have found to be most helpful when encountering biblical imagery: critical biblical studies, the application of imaginal spirituality, and feminist thought.

> *From Augustine's* Confessions, *in the fifth century:*
>
> Too late have I loved you,
> O Beauty so ancient and so new.[2]

Objective Figures of Speech in Psalm 18

Many contemporary Christians are accustomed to imagining God as similar to humans. So God has eyes and speaks words and works like a shepherd. Yet biblical and historic divine figures of speech include a substantial number of figures of speech that are objective, that is, that liken God to an object. Chapter 2 has demonstrated one of the primary objective figures for God: that God is like fire, even that God "is" fire. This chapter begins by examining, verse by verse, the figures of speech in Psalm 18, as rendered in the Revised Standard Version of the Bible. Psalm 18 has been selected because of its wide range of both objective and anthropomorphic imagery, taken from nature, society, warfare, and Israelite history.[3]

strength (v. 1) Although this psalm is mainly about God's salvation of the chosen people, in this text God is always "my" God, "my strength": the historical legends concerning the victories of Israel have become the creed of the worshiping individual.

rock (v. 2) The reference here is not to some small precious stone that we might hold in our hands, but rather to the high rock faces in Palestine in which are caves that provided protection from attack and cliffs that offered a lookout during warfare in the Ancient Near East. We might picture ourselves hiding within the towering sandstone masterpieces in Arizona's Monument Valley. Looking to a rock to protect us during battle fits well with this psalm's focus on victory over enemies.

fortress (v. 2) This figure of speech assumes the likelihood of violent assault. The psalms assume continuous troubles afflicting humankind, and fortress suggests a shelter in which I will need to seek refuge. But note the opposite in verse 29, in which God helps us to leap over a wall to freedom. If we need protection, God is fortress, and if we are imprisoned inside walls, God is our means of escape. No single figure of speech for God is sufficient: each figure of speech is best balanced by its opposite.

shield (v. 2) In ancient warfare, shields were an essential means of protection, keeping assault away from one's body. We hold God in front of our bodies, cowering behind God, and so are protected. Our troops, standing side by side behind a wall of shields, can advance fearlessly toward the enemy.

From Thomas Troeger, a hymn in the twentieth century:

Source and Sovereign, Rock and Cloud,
Fortress, Fountain, Shelter, Light,
Judge, Defender, Mercy, Might,
Life whose life all life endowed. . .[4]

horn of my salvation (v. 2) Biblical scholars debate what this horn is. It may refer to the animal horns that were attached to the Ark of the Covenant, to assist those who carried the sacred chest from place to place. Such animal horns, aside from providing handholds, would have signified the victorious power of the male. It may also be that grabbing hold of these horns ensured personal safety from attack, as we see in the medieval idea that touching the altar granted sanctuary to those escaping arrest. For some interpreters, the horn suggests instead the shofar, the ram's horn blown to signify significant religious and social events in Israelite life. ***Question:*** *When praying this psalm, does it matter that we do not know what this horn is referring to?*

stronghold (v. 2) We might think not only of the military protection provided by the height of a fortification, but also of the stronghold of the parent hugging the child or the companion embracing the loved one with compassion and care.

support (v. 18) Many people in our society resist the supports called for in old age or infirmity, disdaining the use of canes or walkers. It is as if we want always to imagine humans as independently strong and upright, as if we do not want even to lay our eyes on such supports. The psalmist praises God for being like the staff of the king, a necessary symbol of monarchal might.

lamp (v. 28) A tamed fire can provide a safe source of light. The king, and we worshipers as well, rely on God as our lamp. In our time of nearly perpetual ambient lighting, this figure of speech may have minimal impact on us.

Next comes a section in which the inexplicable tumults of nature manifest God. Earthquake (v. 7), volcano (8), darkness (9), wind (10), hail (12), thunder (13), lightning (14), storm at sea (15): all these natural phenomena are the figures of speech invoked to describe God. We are accustomed to speaking of God seen in a gorgeous sunset, but not so much in a tsunami. ***Question:*** *What is your reaction to the current practice of insurance companies that avoid reimbursing the stricken by referring to natural catastrophes as "acts of God"?*

Anthropomorphic Figures of Speech in Psalm 18

LORD (v. 1) = As throughout the Hebrew Bible, in Psalm 18 God is named LORD. We are accustomed to naming God as LORD. Yet this circumlocution for the name of God is itself a layered figure of speech. LORD is the traditional Christian way in the English language to render YHWH, the tetragrammaton that signifies the personal Hebrew name of God, which was perhaps "Yahweh." In rendering YHWH as LORD, God's given name has been replaced with a cultural title of authority. If the "lords" in one's society are known for justice and beneficence, the title serves our faith well. If, on the other hand, we associate lordship with the worst in human governance or if we even reject the very idea of lordship, this classic figure of speech is sadly inadequate for believers. Often in the prophetic literature God is called "the LORD of hosts." Most likely, the original meaning of "hosts" referred to God's angelic armies, and perhaps later meant the planets and stars, that is, the hosts of the heavenly skies, and later still, the nine ranks of angels. ***Question:*** *What should we do with "LORD"?*

deliverer (v. 2) In spite of continuous warfare, the believing community credits God with delivery from defeat. For the many who know only defeat, this figure of speech might encapsulate hope.

> *From the memoirs of Perpetua, martyred in the second century:*
>
> I saw a garden of great proportions. A tall man with white hair, who was dressed as a shepherd, was in the midst of the garden milking sheep. He said, "My child, you are welcome." Then he gave me some of the milk from his milking, which I held in my cupped hands and drank.[5]

Most High (v. 13) The resident Canaanites worshiped El, that is, the supreme God. El was granted various qualifiers at different sanctuaries, the qualifier used in Jerusalem being El Elyon, "God Most High." Studying the Old Testament, we ought not imagine some comprehensive change among Israelites from one religious practice to another, but rather decades, even centuries, of the movement from polytheism to monotheism, from image veneration to iconoclasm. Here we see Israelites appropriating this pagan designation of God, which may suggest that God is "up," from earlier Canaanite usage, and this title gets attached especially to the idea of divine judgment.

Next comes a section in which ancient warfare provides figures of speech for God. Here the anthropomorphisms for God are embedded in the verb. So God trains me for war (v. 34), provides me instruments of war (35), girds me for battle (39), turns away assailants (39), subdues enemies (47), and delivers me from those who are violent (48). God is the commander of our armies, granting triumph, because God loves our anointed king (v. 50). For the worshiping Christian in the twenty-first century, these figures of speech from archaic military vocabulary might find meaning also in our own world, for we indeed face violence in our nation or watch wars being waged the world over. Whether in our community or within our very self, there is destructive conflict, and the ancient military imagery might assist our prayer. But for some Christians, these military figures of speech are reprehensible and ought to be discarded, since they appear to authorize national self-serving violence. ***Question:*** *Can you suggest a political scenario in which Christians can, indeed must, see God as leading warfare against evil?*

Finally in Psalm 18 God is lauded as active to save, as rewarding good behavior and punishing evil. So God rebukes (v. 15), delights in me (19), rewards me (20), and recompenses me (24). ***Question:*** *How close or how distant from your spirituality is the religious conviction that God rewards the faithful?*

Objective Figures of Speech from Throughout the Bible

Moving beyond Psalm 18, we find many more objective figures of speech for God throughout the Bible. Here are some:

cloud (Exod. 16:10) We understand "a cloud" to be a mass of water that is visible above the earth and "the cloud" to be a global network of digital data. In the Bible, a cloud is usually the sign of the presence of God. Perhaps for some ancient worshipers, residing in a desert climate, a cloud as the promise of rain was something of the literal presence of God. ***Question:*** *How could the digital cloud also be a sign of the presence of God?*

> *From Mechthild of Magdeburg, in the thirteenth century:*
>
> O you burning Mountain, O you chosen Sun,
> O you full Moon, O you bottomless Well,
> O you unscalable Height, O you Brightness without measure,
> O Wisdom without ground, O Mercy without restraint,
> O Might without opposition, O Crown of all honors!
> The most humble person you ever created praises you.[6]

cup (Ps 16:5) This figure of a shared cup is particularly appropriate for Christian use, given the cup of wine shared in the eucharist. Those Christians who refrain from using a common cup may miss an original intention of this figure of speech.

diadem (Isa 28:5) God will be a crown of beauty for the people. The fifteenth-century mystic Julian of Norwich reverses this image when she says that we are God's crown.[7]

dwelling place (Ps. 90:1) It is as if we reside in God, as if not only the believer but also the entire cosmos rests within the divine. Since we no longer assert that God resides above the earth, it might be comforting to imagine God as the outside perimeter of all things.

eagle (Deut 32:11–12) Many Christians know this figure of speech well as it is cited in hymns and popular spiritual songs. An eagle is a powerful bird of prey famed for its extraordinary vision, and the mother eagle is lauded for her practice of flying with outstretched wings beneath her fledglings, to catch them if they founder. The eagle became a common symbol also for the fourth evangelist, whose Gospel account is said to see farther than do the synoptic evangelists and thus to speak most profoundly of God.

fountain (Ps 36:9) Christians have cited this figure of speech in their consideration of baptism, for which the water of baptism is lauded as the source and nurture of the Christian life.

heaven (Matt 4:17) The Gospel according to Mark repeatedly speaks of "the kingdom of God" (Mark 1:15). A decade later, the Gospel according to Matthew, its text directed more clearly for a Jewish audience, has changed that to "the kingdom of heaven." This change introduces to many contemporary minds the mental image of a place called "heaven," in which God reigns and the angels reside and, perhaps, boasts streets of gold. Since in the Scriptures "the heavens" is usually a designation for the sky and for the universe outside and beyond the earth, the Matthean usage seems to have provided, not a reference to a location above the earth in which God dwells but more a circumlocution for "God," that is, a figure of speech helpful for those Jewish believers who were hesitant to speak with ease of "God." Thus, the believers' expression "that at death we go to heaven" might mean to say, using Matthew's speech, that at death, we go to God. It may be that too much Christian expectation of life in heaven after death misses the point of life with God here and now. ***Question:*** *What do you think the evangelist Matthew would say about this?*

> *From Herbert F. Brokering's "Thine the Amen," in the twentieth century:*
>
> Thine the glory in the night no more dying only light
> thine the river thine the tree then the Lamb eternally
> then the holy holy holy celebration jubilee
> thine the splendor thine the brightness only thee only thee.[8]

hiding place (Ps 32:7) Also this figure of speech seems to be rooted in the desire for protection in wartime. Yet children throughout the globe play games in which they hide from one another.

I AM (Exod 3:14) This rendering of the enigmatic name of God offers us an image of being, of unbounded life beyond what humans know in themselves, the Living One other than human. Some biblical scholars view I AM as the single enduring name of God, and worshipers will encounter it in several favored hymns.[9] Since in several places in the Gospel according to John, and arguably also in Mark, this figure of speech occurs in relation to Christ, we will look at it again in chapter 4.

light (Ps 27:1) In the poetic account of creation in Genesis 1, God creates light before creating the sun. Thus often in the Bible light indicates the presence of God, rather than being a natural feature of the solar system.

portion (Ps 16:5) When settling in Palestine the Israelite tribe of Levi was given primary roles in the worship life of Jerusalem, rather than the ownership of an allotment of land. The figure of speech that God is one's portion suggested to the Israelite contentment with one's placement in the land mass and among the communal roles of the whole people. The use of "portion" as a figure of speech for God exemplifies the conundrum question of translation: how much should an archaic word be rendered in a culturally accessible term, versus how much should Christians be taught to know and use biblical speech.

refuge (Ps 14:6) Originally this figure of speech suggested God's protection from military assault. In our time, we might think of refugees from war, oppression, poverty, or prejudice seeking refuge, or ourselves as desiring personal security.

shade (Ps 121:5) The intensity of the sun can kill. Humans require shade.

shadow of your wings (Ps 17:8) In the iconography of ancient Egypt, beings with divine power were depicted with immense wings that overspread the earth. For example, the Egyptian goddess of justice, Maat, is shown with overshadowing wings. Also in Hebrew poetry, God's mighty wings are over all. ***Question:*** *Do God's wings help you pray?*

silence (1 Kgs 19:12) In the Bible, God speaks. Continuously. And in ancient poetic expressions, God thunders and roars. So it is a surprise that here God is "heard" in silence. For many believers, that God is present as silence is a particularly consoling figure of speech.

sun (Ps 84:11) God is shade, God is sun. Many figures of speech are the surprising opposite of other figures of speech.

tower (Ps 61:3) Also this image was originally part of a city's fortification, a lookout in protection of advancing enemies. The beloved eighth-century Irish hymn "Be thou my vision" calls God "my high tower," and so we might imagine God as the impressive early medieval towers that dot the Irish countryside.[10]

wind (Jer 18:17) An example of how complex is the task of biblical translation is the Hebrew noun *ruah,* which can be translated breath, spirit, or wind. Thus in Genesis 1:2, the translator could accurately render *ruah* as either a breath, a spirit, or a wind from God that hovers over the waters. ***Question:*** *How would you prefer that Genesis 1:2 be rendered in modern English?*

Anthropomorphic Figures of Speech from Throughout the Bible

The great monotheistic religions of Judaism, Christianity, and Islam all agree that God is transcendent, without a literal body, and each religious tradition has developed its own methods for indoctrinating its followers in this belief. Yet Christianity has developed a complex pattern of speech that might be seen as negating its very theological principles: that is, the Scriptures and the tradition are filled with memorable expressions that assert that God is indeed like a being with a human body. Nearly all interpreters of biblical texts recognize that this speech is metaphoric language, and that although utilizing figures of speech that apply a human body to God, thoughtful writers and expositors of the Jewish and Christian traditions did not take such imagery literally. It has recently, however, been argued, against all extant Christian theological writings, that bodily descriptions of God ought to be seen as originally having been literally believed. Not even in the past, goes this argument, was metaphor ever intended. From this point of view, one must say that the literal God of the Bible has been killed off and is no longer honored.[11] Rejecting the role of metaphor, such a believer might assert that God is both existing as transcendent and possessing a literal body, which comes to expression in Jesus of Nazareth.[12] Yet the Bible's interplay of figures of speech, the weaving together of a variety of images, suggests

> *From John Thornburg, "God, the Sculptor of the Mountains," in the twentieth century:*
>
> God the sculptor of the mountains,
> God the miller of the sand,
> God the jeweler of the heavens,
> God the potter of the land:
> you are womb of all creation,
> we are formless; shape us now.[13]

that even the ancient poets were aware of their use of metaphor. ***Question:*** *Which bodily descriptions of God do you find helpful in your prayer and praise?*

Readers encounter two anthropomorphisms in the very first pages of the Bible. In the first story of creation, God establishes the sabbath rest, not out of sheer divine power but because God wanted to rest after the exertion of creation (Gen 2:2), and in the second story of creation, God was "walking in the garden at the time of the evening breeze" (Gen 3:8). To rest and to take a walk: such a deity resembles humans. As well, God has breath (Job 33:4); ears (Ps 130:2); eyes (Deut 11:12); nostrils (Exod 15:8); a mouth (Deut 8:3); a voice (Ps 29:4); a finger (Exod 31:18); a right hand (Ps 18:35); and feet (Exod 24:10). ***Question:*** *Do these anthropomorphisms assist or disturb your worship?*

mighty hand and an outstretched arm In this phrase, repeated many times in the Old Testament, God is described as acting for the people, and as if with a human, it is God's strong hand and extended arm that are lauded.

a back In Exodus 33:20–23 is the remarkable account of Moses asking to see God, and God stipulating that only God's backside can be seen. Moses is to hide in the cleft of a rock: Christians are meant to recall this story when singing the hymn

"Rock of ages, cleft for me, let me hide myself in thee."[14] It has been suggested that God's "back" is what follows after God, that is, the effect of God's relationality with humans.[15]

a face Yet in several other places, such as Exodus 33:11, God and Moses did see each other face to face, and in the blessings in Numbers 6:25–26, God's face will shine upon all the people. Some Christians have interpreted this Aaronic blessing as referring to the Trinity, God the Father as keeper, God's face seen in Jesus Christ the Son, and God the Spirit as peace-giver.

The passage in Isaiah 66:11 that speaks of "her consoling breast, her glorious bosom" is referring to the city of Jerusalem. Until recent decades, it was commonplace in many languages to refer to a city with the feminine gender. It was as if the city, female, welcomed the presence of the god, male. Isaiah employs this figure of speech, which construes the city, not God, as female. When the word "breast" appears in traditional hymnody, the reference seems to be an asexual term for "chest." In the Judeo-Christian tradition, the creative power of God rests in God's word, not in any part of God's body. It is instructive of the tradition's practice of distancing God's body from sexuality that in the Scriptures, the biblical God has no womb, no penis, no sexual or reproductive organs.

Yet in medieval mystics, we encounter lush praise of the milk from God's breast as a descriptor of the wine of communion. Some recent hymnody refers to God's womb, perhaps capitalizing on the connection in Hebrew between *rechem*, which means womb, and *rachum,* which means mercy, and that thus "Motherly Father" is a welcome divine designation.[16] We shall attend to this issue more fully in chapter 5. Interestingly, in neither the Scriptures nor the tradition is found comparable male imagery of bodily reproduction. ***Question:*** *Why is it more acceptable to imagine and depict naked women than naked men?*

Here we can only briefly mention other ways that God is described anthropomorphically. God is described as exhibiting anger (Exod 4:14), compassion (Deut 13:17), love (1 John 4:16), regret (Gen 6:6). Occasionally (see Ps 35:22–23), the text suggests that the reason God is not acting to save the people is that God is sleeping. In yet more anthropomorphisms, God "changed his mind," (Jon 3:10), is jealous (Deut 5:9), laughs (Ps 2:4), albeit in this passage the laughter intends scorn.

Here are yet more anthropomorphic figures of speech for the biblical God.

Abba (Gal. 4:6) Paul writes to the Galatians in the mid first century, that, having been adopted as God's children and having been given the Spirit of Christ, they are to address God as Abba. That the Gospel according to Mark cites Jesus in Gethsemane as calling God Abba (Mark 14:36), when the narrative suggests that there were no witnesses to Jesus's prayer, suggests that Jesus was remembered as addressing God with this endearment. Over the last few decades there has been considerable discussion of the precise meaning of this term and its history in Christian worship. A twenty-first-century prayer book entitled *Abba, Amma* adds the motherly to the fatherly parent.[17] ***Question:*** *When ought adults to pray as if they are children?*

Ancient One (Dan 7:9) Known to many Christians by an older translation—the Ancient of Days—this figure of speech claims the Israelite deity as prior to, and thus more authoritative, than the neighboring deities. For those contemporary Christians who are attracted only to what is new, the Ancient One provides a balance by stretching time back into the past.

avenger (Ps 99:8) Thus believers can hope that the wicked will be punished and the oppressed be vindicated and avenged.

builder (Heb 3:4) The author of Hebrews calls God the builder of all things. Thus arises the question whether God built also the instruments of evil.

creator (Isa 40:28, Isa 43:15) Sometimes God is praised as the creator of the known universe, and other times as the creator of the people of Israel.

father (Ps 103:13) The several times in the Hebrew Bible that God is referred to as father reflect the common understanding in the Ancient Near East that the king was a son of the god or the goddess who then received authority from that deity. Although in some passages, because of the role of the king as a Son of God, the whole nation can call God father (Isa 63:16, Isa 64:8), it is mainly King David who is understood as "Son of God." See for example Psalm 89, in which God chooses David and anoints him king, who then "shall cry to me, 'You are my Father' " (v. 26, also Ps 2:7). In Matthew 6:9, Jesus instructs his followers to pray to God as "our father in heaven" and in Luke 11:2 as father. Through the decades of the composition of the four Gospels, "father" became increasingly the primary figure of speech for God, with an original meaning more political than familial, more social than personal. Chapter 4 will expand on the figure of Jesus as God's son.

friend (Jer 3:4) Christians have become accustomed to this welcoming divine figure of speech, which presents a stark contrast to many deities of other ancient cultures.

guide (Ps 48:14) In faith, Christians recognize God as their guide, although direct or personal influence from God is not always evident.

helper (Ps 54:4) Usually we think of a helper as someone secondary to the task, one who assists the person who is responsible for the task. Here God takes this secondary role.

Holy One (Hos 11:9) In our time, the adjective "holy" suggests sinlessness. In biblical parlance, it suggested instead the otherness of God, God's utter transcendence.

husband (Jer 31:32) A traditional way that Western languages described a city was in female terminology and, correspondingly, the reigning deity as a male centered in the city. According to this usage. Jerusalem is a she, the submissive wife, and God is a he, the dominant husband. An inclusive way to represent this marital bond in our time is to say that God has married the people.

judge (Ps 7:11) Israelite judges could be either male or female, and the expectation was that they ensured justice for the oppressed in the community. Since the activity of judges preceded the dissemination of written law codes, the society trusted that judges exercised wisdom that had been granted them from God.

keeper (Ps 121:5) To Julian of Norwich in the fifteenth century, the Trinity is our keeper.[18]

king (Ps 5:2) 1 Samuel 8 is a masterpiece of commentary on the reality of monarchy. As the tribes of Israel develop into a monarchy, the prophet Samuel predicts the many distressing features of the power of a king. Furthermore, in the Bible as in much world history, the reigns of queens are judged far more harshly than that of kings. For many contemporary British citizens, the monarchy, largely because it stands outside politics, can serve as a positive symbol of national unity and honor, yet for many contemporary Americans, monarchs are seen as affecting more harm than good, and the archaic practice ought to cease. ***Question:*** *Does residence in a nation with a monarchy substantially influence how this figure of speech functions for the worshiping Christian?*

lawgiver (Jas 4:12) Sometimes the biblical reference to "law" means to point to the Torah, sometimes to wider human statutes of conduct. This figure of speech has been important for some Christian spiritualities, but not for all. "Law" might suggest something very different for those Christians who can make the laws, as distinct from those who must merely obey them.

master/mistress (Ps 123:2) In the similes in this short and gentle psalm we encounter a dual gendered figure of speech, rare in the Bible.

mother (Isa 66:13) Here God, like the city, mothers the people. For Julian of Norwich, it is the Second Person who mothers her.

potter (Isa 64:8) Depending on the culture, either males or females functioned as potters, fulfilling an essential role of providing containers for the people's food and water.

protector (Ps 68:5) Even religious leaders are guilty of abuse and assault. Thus not everyone experiences protection from God's emissaries.

savior (Luke 1:47) From what do we hope that God will save us? Many Christians no longer fear hell, but we can rejoice to be saved from our small and selfish selves.

shepherd (Ps 23:1) In the pastoral cultures of the Ancient Near East, as well as in more recent times, young unmarried women joined with their brothers to serve as shepherds. Children's books with creative illustrations may assist in widening the imagery of shepherd to include women.[19]

sovereign (Ps 8:1) In the parlance of the United States, the people are the sovereign. In the psalms, the sovereign is God. ***Question:*** *Do the nongendered nouns "sovereign" or "monarch" alter in any way one's reception of the biblical imagery of kingship?*

wisdom (Prov 3:13–18, 8:1–9:6) Here and in several other places in the Hebrew Bible, God is called wisdom, in several places personified as a powerful immortal female who assisted God in creation and who rears the people in the ways of truth and righteousness. There is considerable scholarly debate concerning the biblical figure of *Hokmah*.[20] Some scholars argue that early Israel did worship a goddess, a female consort for a male god Yahweh. Other scholars maintain that this image is a literary convention within a male academic community, in which goodness is described as Woman Wisdom and evil as Dame Folly. Some Christians have been glad of a restored use of Wisdom as a female image of divinity, while others are upset by what they perceive as contemporary goddess worship. In Christian usage, Woman Wisdom most often has been applied to the Second Person of the Trinity, which chapter 4 addresses.

woman in labor (Isa 42:14) Here God is likened to a woman crying out in labor pains. As with the hope for a human woman in labor, also God's agony can bring forth life.

woman sweeping (Luke 15:8) In Luke 15 there is the parable of the shepherd searching for the last sheep, followed by the parable of the woman searching her home for a lost coin. If the shepherd is a figure of speech for God, so is the woman sweeping her house.

Some biblical passages include no noun as a succinct descriptor for God, but the figure of speech must be inferred. God is a combative wrestler (Gen 32:24–30) who both bests and blesses Jacob. Like an ancient deity, God slays the primordial monster (Ps 74:13–14). Like a mother, God "bore you . . . gave you birth" (Deut 32:18). Each of these passages is exceptional to the usual pattern in the Hebrew Bible, in which God is described as active historically, rather than mythically.

Objective Figures of Speech from Christians Past and Present

Of the countless innovative objective figures of speech that Christians have proposed when addressing and describing God, here are some.

air enveloping the whole globe of being[21] For the twentieth-century American poet Denise Levertov, God is as the air, the unseen necessity for life, not only of the globe of the earth, but also of the globe of all being.

ark[22] Throughout church history, the ark has often served as a figure of speech for the church, sailing through the waters of baptism to safety, but the eighteenth-century poet Ann Griffiths names God our Ark.

circle, first and last and altogether[23] The sixteenth-century clergyman and poet John Donne called God a circle, and then called God "a direct line," leading us from our beginning to our end. ***Question:*** *Which figure of speech is most helpful to you, God as circle or God as line?*

darkness[24] Already in the fifth century, the mystic we call Pseudo-Dionysius knew God as transcendent darkness. In the twenty-first century, some hymnwriters have revived this image, realizing the insufficiency of imagery which identifies God solely as light.

firmament, roof for my head[25] The twentieth-century Medical Mission Sister Miriam Therese Winter was an early proponent of Christian hymns that relied on imagery other than male imagery. We tend to imagine space, not a roof, above us. Perhaps God as a roof is more comforting.

force[26] This phrase translated from Hildegard of Bingen has been made into the opening line of the hymn "I Am That Great and Fiery Force." The hymn goes on to quote one of Hildegard's favorite usages, "greening" as a sign of divine power.

garden[27] This figure of speech is found in an anonymous text surviving from the first few generations of Christians. God is not only a field in which food is grown but also a delightful garden that was planted with the intention to please.

ground of being[28] One of the premier theologians of the twentieth century, Paul Tillich, speaking Christian faith in the language of existentialism, wrote that God is other than merely "a being," which he said diminishes God. Rather, God is the very ground of being, being itself.

healing river[29] The flowing fresh waters of a river bring healing to wounds, and God is such a healing river. Some Christians continue the ancient practice of baptism in flowing rivers, and those who use an indoor font describe even its small amount of water as a healing river.

my heart's desire[30] A praise chorus that paraphrases Psalm 42:1 calls God "my heart's desire." ***Question:*** *Do we actually want God above all else?*

home[31] In his 1804 ode "Intimations of Immortality," the British poet William Wordsworth articulated his belief in the immortality of the soul when citing "God, who is our home."

journey and the journey's end[32] Recently the age-old image of life as a journey has become important for some Christians, especially given that many contemporary individuals can travel between quite different life experiences. Many churches have constructed an exterior or interior labyrinth to provide a space for ritualized journeys. From Boethius, the sixth-century philosopher, comes a prayer in which God is not only the journey (we travel in God) but also the terminus (we go to God).

From Francis Quarles, "The Loadstone," in the seventeenth century:

Eternal God! O Thou that only art
The sacred fountain of eternal light,
And blessed loadstone of my better part,
O Thou my heart's desire, my soul's delight![33]

lighthouse[34] Describing the Christian life, this figure of speech in the gospel song "My Lighthouse" assumes that the troubled sea is wild and the night is dark, and only in God is there the promise of arrival in the safety of the shore. However, in this song by the Rend Collective, I would change all the "my" to "our."

mirror[35] In the middle of the twentieth century, the Roman Catholic Romano Guardini published exquisite descriptions of the spirituality of Christian liturgy. In this prayer, he calls God his holy mirror in whom lies our dignity and our honor.

path[36] The sixth-century monk Columba, instrumental in the establishment of the monastery at Iona, is remembered as calling God "a smooth path below me." The implication is that one is always liable to fall and, given the ancient parlance that what is below is hell and the realm of the dead, that God is the path below me is a comforting idea.

sea without a shore, a sun without a sphere[37] The seventeenth-century British Anglican priest John Mason composed many hymns, but eventually lost his mind to the idea that Christ's second coming had already occurred. In the poem "How shall I sing that majesty," the poet is nearly overwhelmed by the presence of God.

From Dan Damon, "Shadow and Substance," in the twentieth century:

Shadow and substance, wonder and mystery,
spell-binding spinner of atoms and earth;
soul of the cosmos, person and energy,
source of our being: we sing of your worth.[38]

star-abiding one[39] "Many and Great, O God, are your works," a hymn that celebrates especially Psalms 102 and 8, was written first in the Dakota language. Its title for God, *Wakantanka*, has been rendered in English as either Great Spirit or Great Mystery and is used by the Lakota peoples to designate the creator God. God has created the stars, and God lives among the stars. In lauding the creation, this hymn situates God primarily above the earth, and asks God to "dwell with us."

In Australia, considerable recent sorrow over the practices of European colonizers has led to some Christian receptivity of Aboriginal religion and its language of "the Dreamtime," and one prayer in an Anglican liturgical book addresses "God of Holy Dreaming, Great Creator Spirit."[40]

uncreated sun[41] This is one of a dozen figures of speech in a seventeenth-century hymn by Johann Scheffler. By making the sun "uncreated" the author has expanded a common image into one unique image.

wound that is a joy[42] For John of the Cross, from whom comes the phrase "the dark night of the soul," the visitation of God the Lover kills the old self and replaces it with sacred holiness. Thus the wound to the self is paradoxically our joy.

Anthropomorphic Figures of Speech from Christians Past and Present

architect of the universe[43] The Presbyterian minister Peter Marshall, who served as the chaplain of the United States Senate from 1947–49, was beloved for the distinctive rhetoric of his prayers. This figure of speech may have been especially meaningful to a legislature that thought of itself as building the world.

author[44] Calling God author focuses on the word, the word of life, the word spoken to God, the word heard from God.

bakerwoman[45] "Strong, brown Bakerwoman God, I am your low, soft, and being-shaped bread" surprises us with its reversal of the figure of speech for the food of the eucharist. Here God is the baker, we are the bread.

Black Woman[46] The title of a 2022 book by Christena Cleveland alerts the reader to the many ways that God is stereotypically thought of as like a white man, and that such thought needs to be transformed by the image of God as a black woman.

friend and enemy[47] In another example of describing God with opposite—even opposing—nouns, the believer is invited to experience the divine in surprising ways. ***Question:*** *How and when do we see God acting as the enemy?*

grandfather[48] Telling the story of the Oglala Sioux, the medicine man Black Elk was quoted as calling the Great Spirit "my grandfather," seen as a title of respect for tradition. ***Question:*** *What are your personal resonances with the word "grandfather"?*

guest and stranger[49] In one of David Adam's Celtic-style poems, God is not only the guest who waits inside but also the stranger at the door. The paradox widens our reception of God's presence.

> *From Timothy J. Mark, in the twentieth century:*
>
> O God, slum-dweller, beggar, cripple, leper –
> O God, without work, hungry, thirsty –
> O God, forsaken, alone –
> help us to know you.[50]

mad lover[51] The fourteenth-century mystic Catherine of Siena understood that she was married to God, who was simultaneously angry at her and wildly in love with her.

mother[52] From their earliest formation, the Christian sect known as the Shakers referred to God as both father and mother. It is instructive that often in church history a sect focused on a single concern that later became more acceptable in the wider church.

owner[53] A Prayer of Thanksgiving appointed for use in the Anglican Church of Kenya called God "owner of all things"—an appropriate figure of speech for Christians emerging from the claims of ownership asserted by past colonial powers.

physician[54] It is common in world religions for the deity to be invoked as physician. Jesus himself was remembered as a faith healer. The intercessions of the assembled Christian community on a Sunday often list the sick by name, thus continuing the age-old plea that God as physician will direct the method of healing.

pilot[55] In the famous poem "Crossing the Bar," perhaps composed as an elegy, the British poet Alfred, Lord Tennyson, describes the end of life as a sea journey, at the culmination of which he finally sees God face to face, the God who was, unbeknownst to him, his pilot all along.

taskmaster[56] In this seventeenth-century sonnet, the Puritan John Milton muses about what has already occurred in his life and what may still come to be, and his tone of peaceful acceptance concludes with the startling figure of speech that God is in fact his taskmaster, a term that many Christians might identify only with the slave drivers of ancient Egypt.

traveler unknown[57] As in the narrative about Easter at Emmaus, when God comes to us, it may be that we do not recognize who God is.

weaver[58] In the second stanza of "Let Streams of Living Justice," Willliam Whitla pleads for justice for the workers. God is called "great weaver of our fabric," and the words loom, thread, bind, texture, and color all build upon the image of weaver. In some cultures, the females were the weavers, and in others, the males.

womb[59] The hymn "O God, Great Womb" composed in 1980 by Harris J. Loewen, is one of several recent hymns that give to God a womb. ***Question:*** *If we are born of God's womb, are humans made of God?*

young, growing God[60] Greek philosophy established in Western religion the idea that since God is perfection, God never changes. Yet twentieth-century Christian theologians have explored the evolutionary idea that, along with the cosmos, also God evolves. Brian Wren presents figures of speech in which God is a strong mother, a warm father, old and aching, young and growing, always "great living God," a God changing constantly for the good of all.

Utilizing Figures of Speech for the First Person of the Trinity

We have seen here a great array of objective and anthropomorphic figures of speech for the First Person of the Trinity. It has recently been argued that anthropomorphic imagery for God is much the best, and the best anthropomorphic terms are kinship titles, such as father and brothers, perhaps also mother. Given the Middle English word *kinde*, and its connection with our words *kin* and *kindness*, it is asserted that kinship categories make clear the reciprocal relationship possible between God and the believer.[61] Since Christianity hopes for a loving relationship between the ineffable God and contingent humans, titles of kinship may make such relationship believable. Yet we must ask whether kinship titles can be compensatory for the countless persons for whom relatives have been uncaring, abusive, or even unknown, and whether the male anthropomorphic figures of speech merely reflect a society in which human males had authority to choose religious language and to order Western society.

> *From Dhuoda of Septimania, in the ninth century, in a letter to her son:*
>
> Believe that God is above you, below you, within, and outside of you, for our God is everywhere, within and without. The Lord is the reality around us because the impregnable wall of God surrounds us all. Take delight in the Lord.[62]

This chapter has raised many questions: What are the gains of anthropomorphic imagery? What are the losses? Can we balance male imagery with female imagery? How shall we speak of nonbinary persons? How helpful is it to imagine God as an immense human? Does human imagery make God a more welcoming and accessible figure? To what degree might this practice actually diminish God, to a being only a bit bigger than ourselves? It is a gift to the worship life of the baptized that we need choose not only one genre of speech. Rather, there is time in the hour of worship and in the lifetime of the believer to intersperse objective imagery with anthropomorphic, classic with innovative.

This chapter has perused a long list of figures of speech for the First Person of the Trinity. We need now to consider how and when Christians can make much use of these figures of speech. Sadly, some Sunday worship relies on only a very few figures of speech for God, and those being anthropomorphic: God as father, as king, as creator. Furthermore, if assembly worship does not model for the faithful the use of dozens of figures of speech, it is not likely that many Christians would invent this practice on their own so as to take advantage of them in their personal prayer. But there are ways that figures of speech for the First Person, whether biblical, historical, or contemporary, can take their rightful place in Christian spirituality.

In the first place, the ecumenical and Roman Catholic three-year lectionaries, by appointing a psalm for each Sunday and festival, offer to Christians a biblical wealth of figures of speech for God. On many Sundays the psalm selection presents several figures of speech in praise and petition to God. These psalms can be chanted by the entire assembly, sung by a choir or a cantor, or versified into a hymn. The psalms ought never be discarded as of minimal importance for worship. Rather, they can be revered as the church's first hymnal, filled with inspired language in poetic form that can teach us an ongoing pattern of divine address.

Second, the practice of the assembly singing at least three hymns at each Sunday worship provides access to a treasury of figures of speech. When the text of hymns that is provided for worshipers indicates the century in which the words were composed, the plethora of figures of speech welcomes current Christians into a history of imaginal worship that can allow historic variations in our own commonplace usage. That several hymns are sung allows for a variation on the imagery of the day, so that, for example, if the lectionary's readings focus on the image of light, at least one of the hymns can praise God as darkness.

> *From Brian Wren, "Bring Many Names," in the twentieth century:*
>
> Great, living God, never fully known,
> joyful darkness far beyond our seeing,
> closer yet than breathing, everlasting home:
> Hail and hosanna, great, living God![63]

The eighth-century hymn "Be Thou My Vision," versified by Eleanor H. Hull, includes twelve different figures of speech for God. The twentieth-century hymn "We Sing to You, O God" by Gracia Grindal combines images from Old Testament stories in which God is rock, shield, and eagle. Some hymns focus on God as creator in innovative ways, such as John Thornburg's 1993 text "God the Sculptor of the Mountains." Some hymns celebrate a single figure of speech, such as the recent hymns "Praise, Praise! You Are My Rock" by Herbert F. Brokering, "On Eagle's Wings" by Michael Joncas, or "O Beauty Ever Ancient" by Shirley Erena Murray. Some address one specific prayer concern, such as Matthäus A. von Löwenstern's seventeenth-century hymn for the nation, "Lord of our Life." George Herbert's memorable poem has been set to music as "Come, My Way, My Truth, My Life." There are as well many hymns in which especially the first stanza attends to imagery appropriate for the First Person of the Trinity.

Third, the presentation of images by print or projection offers another possibility for employing figures of speech for the divine. So, for example, if the lectionary's readings feature water, images of either a mighty waterfall or of a desert-dweller kneeling by the local well to fill her jug can enlarge the figure of water. If the biblical readings describe God as food, both a photo of a farmers' market and a depiction of what that assembly uses as the bread and wine of communion could be shown. If the readings say that God has married the people, pictures of wedding ceremonies in other cultures are a suggestion. Care must be taken, however, when considering the presentation of God as a bearded old white man, since this image is too readily literalized by some of the faithful, thus turning a figure of speech into an idol.

Fourth, we can make creative use of the intercessions. In the Western tradition of intercessory prayer, the baptized community addresses the Trinity by directing liturgical prayer to the Father, through the Son, in the Spirit. Maintaining this tradition, the Sunday intercessions can continue to address the First Person of the Trinity in a series of petitions, but each petition can be enhanced with a figure of speech. Thus, in praying for the church universal, God can be called Rock of safety, Temple of holiness, or Ship of salvation; in praying for the well-being of creation, God can be imagined as the Rainbow of promise, the Tree of Life, or Breath of power; in praying for justice and peace in the nations of the world, God can be petitioned as a mighty Fortress, Sovereign of righteousness, or Peacemaker; in praying for those who are poor or oppressed in any way, God is a Castle, Liberator, or the Everlasting Arms; in praying for all who suffer, God can be called Haven, or Mother, or Healer of our every ill; in praying for local and individual needs, God can be called Treasure or Lover or Friend; and, finally, in thanking God for the lives of those who have died in the faith, God can be called Home or Companion or Guide. The Afterword of this book offers more suggestions about figures of speech used in intercessory prayer. ***Question:*** *In intercessory prayer, can the First Person ever be Fire?*

> *From Jane Parker Huber, "God, Creation's Great Designer," in the twentieth century:*
>
> God, creation's great designer, architect, and artisan,
> Dreamer, builder, and refiner—how we marvel at your plan.[64]

Of course, preachers can find in many of the Sunday readings biblical figures of speech that might be amplified during the sermon.[65] Furthermore, an explanation of a figure of speech found in the day's readings could constitute the focus of an age-appropriate catechetical children's sermon. In these ways, Christians young and old, whether recently baptized or with decades of worship experience, can experience their lives enriched by the biblical images of a God beyond their knowing, outside their own imagination.

This chapter has focused on those figures of speech that describe and address the First Person of the Trinity. In the speech and perhaps also the minds of some Christians, the First Person functions as the whole of God. But we must move along to consider three other sets of figures of speech: next comes the Second Person of the Trinity.

4

THE SECOND PERSON, FIGURATIVELY SPEAKING

Truly Divine and Truly Human

IN EXAMINING THE many figures of speech with which Christians have addressed and described the First Person of the Trinity, chapter 3 paid considerable attention to the practice of anthropomorphisms that over the centuries have been assigned to a transcendent deity. God, who has no physical body, is described as if God did indeed have such a body. Now, as we examine the figures of speech for the Second Person of the Trinity, we find the situation reversed. Christians believe that the transcendent God became incarnate in Jesus of Nazareth. For Christians, the Second Person did indeed have a body, and in a way still does. Thus for the Second Person, human depictions are not metaphoric anthropomorphisms, but are rather the articulation of belief in the incarnation. A primary presenting issue for the Second Person is whether, as the humanity of Jesus is accepted

> *From John Newton, in "How Sweet the Name of Jesus Sounds," in the eighteenth century:*
>
> Dear name! The rock on which I build,
> my shield and hiding place,
> my never-failing treasury, filled
> with boundless stores of grace:
> O Jesus, shepherd, guardian, friend,
> my prophet, priest and king,
> my lord, my life, my way, my end,
> accept the praise I bring.[1]

and lauded, the divinity of the Godhead is also honored. ***Question:*** *For you, is Jesus God?*

It can be said that the divinity of Jesus was more celebrated in centuries past than in the present. The Lucan narrative of the presentation of Jesus in the temple (Luke 2:22–38), appointed in the three-year ecumenical lectionaries for the First Sunday of Christmas year B, is one example. Recent preaching tends to use this narrative to proclaim the humanity of Jesus, an infant member of the human family, carried in his mother's arms to undertake a religious ritual.[2] Yet the classic Eastern Orthodox icon of the Lukan narrative shows the old woman Anna holding a scroll or a tablet on which is summarized her speaking, as Luke records, "about the child to all who were looking for the redemption of Jerusalem." The words on her scroll, translated into English, are "This child has created heaven and earth."[3] The icon invites the believer, while seeing the helpless infant, to encounter the almighty God.

The repository of Christmas carols provides other examples. In the nineteenth-century carol "Away in a Manger," the "sweet" helpless infant lies sleeping in the manger, so passive that he is not even crying.[4] Although the hymn says that Jesus is now looking down from the sky, there is no hint that this infant has created the sky. Yet an earlier hymn, the fourth-century "Of the Father's Love Begotten," calls the child the Alpha and Omega, the source and the ending, the world's redeemer, conceived miraculously as divine and human, lauded by ancient seers and prophets.[5] The refrain "evermore and evermore" stresses the immortality of Christ and of the church's belief in him. It is good in expressing the mystery of Christ that assemblies can sing both of these hymns.

This chapter will cite and discuss about eighty figures of speech for the Second Person, those found in the Bible, in the historic practice of animal imagery, in several hymn stanzas replete with images, and finally from a diversity of Christians past and present. We begin by considering the many figures of speech for the Second Person in the Gospel according to John. It is in part thanks to the wealth and breadth of the fourth Gospel's Christological imagery that the early church symbolized John as the eagle, the evangelist that flies highest and sees farthest of the four.[6]

Figures of Speech from the Gospel According to John

> *From Chaim Potok, in* My Name is Asher Lev, *as the Hasidic Jewish mother explains to her son the museum's paintings of the crucifixion:*
>
> "The goyim believe that he was the moshiach. The goyim believe he was the son of the Ribbono Shel Olom." "What does that mean, the son of the Ribbono Shel Olom?" "I don't begin to understand it."[7]

Son of God (1:49) = Although "Son of God" is not the first figure of speech for the Second Person that is cited in the Gospel according to John, since it became the most significant Christological title, we will consider it first. Indeed, because it became the primary designation for Jesus and a key to the naming of the Trinity, it is difficult to realize that it is, after all, a figure of speech.[8] That Jesus is called Son of God resembles an immense structure, each story built upon the lower story, the basement often ignored, and some Christians visiting only their favorite floor and dashing past all the others on the elevator. It is important to clarify at the outset that we are now thinking in contemporary English, in which proper nouns are capitalized. Thus to many believers, Jesus is the Son of God, not the son of god.

The foundation of this structure we are imagining is found in the Ancient Near Eastern kingship myth, according to which the primary deity, who resides above the sky, has appointed and anointed a regent to rule on earth, who is vested with divine authority. The king reigns by divine right and is lauded as the son of the god. Built on top of this myth is the establishment of Israel as a monarchy, during which, as we see for example in Psalm 2:7 and Psalm 89:25–27, the king of Israel was understood as a son of YHWH. The loss of Israelite national independence led to a further development—the second story of this building?—in which texts praying for the restitution of Jewish sovereignty included references to the hope that God would once again reign through a newly anointed Davidic monarch. ***Question:*** *What would happen to Christian faith if we stopped capitalizing "son"?*

Some records of the Jesus movement suggest that for God's reign to be established, a political revolution would be necessitated; other records seem already more poetic than literal, that in some new eschatological way God's messiah would ensure freedom for the people. Each of the various writings in the New Testament gives more or less focus on the language of Christ as the Son of God. Through the early centuries of the church, the familial titles of father, brother, and sister were increasingly adopted within the community, all of them being elaborations of the idea of Jesus as the firstborn son. The categories of Father and Son became enshrined in the Trinitarian creeds. In later centuries, devotion to Mary, the popularity of the stories of Jesus's birth, and the importance of the doctrine of the virgin birth contributed to a literalization of the language of Jesus as the Son of God, since without a human father, Jesus was somehow even genetically the son of God. Medieval explications of the theory of atonement relied on the relationship between the divine Father and the divine Son. However, on a higher floor of our doctrinal high-rise came critical psychological analyses of these familial categories.

Meanwhile, there came to be an addition to this building that we are imagining, a sort of balcony affixed to each floor. Memories of the prayer life of Jesus, who addressed God in a surprisingly intimate manner, led Christians to join with Jesus in praying to God as Abba. If God is Father, Jesus is the Son of God. Despite the novelty of this figure of speech within Judaism, it was in fact commonplace in ancient patriarchal polytheisms, in which for example Zeus was the father of Apollo, Hermes, Dionysius, Hercules, and others. Believers calling Jesus the Son of God hoped to evangelize Roman citizens, for whom the emperor had acquired the title of Son of God.

A floor near the top of this structure dealt with history's cultural changes, in which fathers and firstborn sons were no longer the foundations of government and society. A higher floor was added by the feminist movement, which challenged the continuing maintenance of this patriarchal speech. As of now, gathered on the rooftop to enjoy the fresh air, Christians in the twenty-first century have not agreed on any primary Trinitarian language for the Second Person that avoids the binary of the Son of the Father. In chapter 6, we shall consider various figures of speech that propose other Trinitarian imagery. ***Question:*** *On which floor of this edifice are you most comfortable?*

Word (1:1) Greek philosophy gave the label Word to the eternal principle of order in the universe, and the Hebrew Scriptures repeatedly cite "the word of the LORD" as the source of the faithful and everlasting creative revelation of God. In calling the Second Person the Word, the church appropriated cultural philosophical language to itself and indicated that the primary place where the Second Person is encountered is the word of the Scriptures.

> *From James Quinn SJ, in "Word of God, Come Down on Earth," in the twentieth century:*
>
> Word eternal, throned on high,
> Word that brought to life creation,
> Word that came from heaven to die,
> crucified for our salvation,
> saving Word, the world restoring,
> speak to us, your love outpouring.[9]

Lamb of God (1:29) Scholars ask whether this early symbol of Christ meant to invoke the suffering servant in Isaiah or to link the crucifixion with the sacrificed paschal lamb. In the fourth Gospel, both simultaneously are possible. In Revelation 5:6, the Lamb is "standing as if it had been slaughtered," thus signaling both the divine and the human.

Rabbi, Teacher (1:38) About half of the Gospel according to John is dedicated to lengthy discourses, teachings spoken by Jesus, interpretations of the Hebrew Scriptures. Part of what distinguishes one Christian denomination from others is the degree to which these teachings of Jesus are granted contemporary authority.

Messiah, the Anointed (1:41) It is the actual anointing, not the ritual of crowning, that signifies the transformation of the heir apparent into the monarch. In the first century, it was salvation by a coming one, anointed by God, that some Jews awaited. In the strange narrative in Mark 14:3–9, Jesus is anointed on his head with costly nard by an unnamed woman at a dinner in the home of "Simon the leper," paradoxically for burial of Jesus's body. But in other passages in the New Testament, the anointing of the Messiah is a figure of speech.

King of Israel (1:49) This title, suggesting that Jesus at his baptism already bears messianic status, recurs in the passion narratives (Mark 15:32, Matt 27:37) in derision. In our day, the State of Israel has added a new referent to which Christians must be attentive.

Son of Man (1:51) This enigmatic title, variously translated as "a son of man," "a human being," or "Son-of-Man," could be used in biblical times self-referentially by any male, but it also designated a mysterious supernatural figure, perhaps an individual, perhaps a personified people of Israel, described in Daniel 7:13–15 and in the intertestamental book of Enoch, who appears in the skies at the end of time as king with everlasting authority. The title appears in all four Gospels, Acts, and Revelation. Jesus is quoted as adopting this title as a self-designation, and it exemplifies the metaphoric nature of figures of speech for Jesus. Here in John 1, the prophecy concerning the Son of Man is layered onto the story of Jacob's ladder (Gen 28:12), thus connecting Jesus with Jacob, who while escaping for his life comes to ensure life for his people. ***Question:*** *How ought we to teach the meaning of the title "Son-of-man"?*

temple (2:19) A temple was understood as an earthly home of a deity, usually featuring an immense statue of the god or goddess and functioning as a locus of worship. In many locations in the Roman Empire, temples to various deities lined the public thoroughfares, and until 70 CE and the destruction of the Jewish temple, life in Jerusalem revolved around temple rituals. In the fourth Gospel, the story of Jesus's cleansing of the temple begins with a literal narrative but concludes metaphorically, to proclaim that Jesus's body is the temple. In this figure of speech, Jesus himself is the home of God and the focus of faithful worship.

serpent (3:14) In this figure of speech, the "Son of Man" is likened to the serpent of Numbers 21:8–9, a faith in which can heal the persons poisoned by snakes. Thus the cross is seen in light of the story of the erected pole, and Jesus as the bronze serpent from whom comes life. Although in Genesis 3 the serpent functions as a personification of evil, in our culture, as with much of antiquity, the caduceus uses the serpent as a sign of healing. Australian Christians know the serpent in Aboriginal myths as the power that, by encircling the globe, holds it together.

I am (6:20, 8:58, 18:6) Repeatedly in the fourth Gospel Jesus asserts his identity with the words *Ego eimi*. In at least these three places, the evangelist seems to intend that Jesus is naming himself "I Am," thus claiming for himself the divine name from Exodus 3:14, "I am who I am," as revealed in the story of the burning bush. It would be helpful if biblical translators did not rely on a footnote to indicate this usage. The Common English Bible, 2011, renders these occurrences of *ego eimi* as "I Am." "Here I AM" is another possible translation in these Johannine passages. "To God and to the Lamb, who is the great I AM" reads one line in the nineteenth-century hymn "What Wondrous Love is This."[10]

> *From "Methinks I see an heavenly host," a medieval Christmas carol:*
>
> The royal Guest you entertain
> Is not of common birth,
> But second in the great I Am,
> The God of heaven and earth.[11]

Lord (6:23) From the earliest Christian writings on, the cultural honorific Lord was applied to Jesus. See, for example, 1 Thessalonians 1:1. Socially, the title was the standard figure of speech for a husband, a leader, or any male authority in the community. Within several decades after the life of Jesus, the title Lord for Jesus merged with LORD, the circumlocution for YHWH. Within several centuries, the creed called also the Spirit "the Lord and Giver of life." In English, the word "lord" was derived from the Anglo-Saxon *hlaf-weard*, the person guarding the bread. Because of this complex linguistic and theological history, some of which relies for clarity on the typography of the printed text, the quest for a replacement title that has no male overtones has been exceedingly difficult.[12]

bread (6:35) Once again, the evangelist turns a literal narrative into a Christological figure of speech. The disciples are seeking bread, and Jesus says that he is the bread.

gate (10:7) For the fourth evangelist, one figure of speech is never enough. So the common biblical metaphor of the divine shepherd is enhanced with the surprising objective image of Christ as a gate that can swing open or closed. Let us pray that it swings open for us.[13]

resurrection (11:25) Once again, the evangelist upends the expected meaning with a divine claim. Martha articulates her faith in God's resurrection of the dead in the eschaton, but Jesus claims that now, here, he is the resurrection. Thus the already complex figure of speech of "the resurrection of the dead" becomes a figure of speech for Jesus Christ. ***Question:*** *What is the resurrection, apart from Jesus Christ?*

vine (15:1) In many places in the Hebrew Bible, the people of Israel are likened to a vine that produces well or poorly. As we have come to expect, the fourth evangelist uses the vine as a figure of speech for Christ, the source of life for all.

way, truth, life (14:6) Centuries of Christian exegetes and hymn-writers have offered various elaborations of the famous phrase, exploring the linkages between the three.

We might conclude this section on the Gospel according to John with an agreement that the fourth evangelist is indeed the church's visionary eagle.

Other Biblical Figures of Speech Applied to the Second Person

wisdom (Prov. 9:1–6) Perhaps a pagan goddess borrowed for literary purposes, perhaps a female manifestation of God honored by some ancient Jews, the depiction of a beautiful transcendent woman in the skies who teaches righteousness and serves a meal of bread and wine became for Christians a figure of speech for the Second Person. It is familiar to us in the Advent hymn "O Come, O Come, Emmanuel," on day two of the sixth-century "O Antiphons," as well as in several recent hymns that expand on the female reference.[14]

> *From Patrick Michaels, in "Who Comes from God," in the twentieth century:*
>
> Who comes from God, as Word and Breath? Holy Wisdom.
> Who holds the keys of life and death? Mighty Wisdom.
> Crafter and Creator, too, Eldest, she makes all things new.
> Wisdom guides what God will do,
> Wisest One, Radiant One, welcome, Holy Wisdom.[15]

servant (Isa 52:13–53:12) Especially the fourth of the Songs of the Servant in Isaiah has been applied by Christians as a dominant figure of speech for the Second Person and might have provided the evangelists with details of the passion and death of Christ, at which they were not physically present. The subject of these poems, the servant, is described as marred in appearance, like root out of dry ground, despised, led to the slaughter like a silent lamb, buried with the wicked, bearing the sins of many, pouring himself out to death.

Emmanuel (Matt 1:23) "God is with us," a title cited in Isaiah 7:14, states that in the coming child is the presence of God. The conclusion to the Gospel according to Matthew restates this figure: "Remember, I am with you always, to the end of the age." ***Question:*** *What do we picture in our minds when hearing the title "Emmanuel"?*

hen (Matt 23:37) In the conclusion of a chapter marked by harsh denunciations of the religious authorities of his day, Jesus likens himself to a mother hen protecting her young. The Filipino hymn by Moises B. Andrade, "When Twilight Comes," elaborates on the figure of Christ as the mother hen.[16] Using classic Lutheran categories, we could say that the mothering hen is the gospel that concludes the law of Matthew's "woes" in chapter 23.

bridegroom (Mark 2:20) The Hebrew Bible often cites the image of the covenant between God and the people as if it were a marriage. Christians borrowed this figure of speech in calling Christ the bridegroom. Especially celibate medieval mystics relished this language and then applied the figure of the bride either to the individual believer or to the church. ***Question:*** *How useful is this male figure of speech in our time?*

cornerstone (Eph 2:20) Expanding the imagery of the church as a building, the author of Ephesians calls Christ Jesus the cornerstone of the church's foundation. Still today a building block can be ritually honored as a symbol of the purpose of a structure.

head (Col 2:19) In Paul's usage, Christ is the whole body of the church. For the author of Colossians, Christ is the head of the body. Figures of speech such as "the body" can be interpreted in alternate ways.

high priest (Heb 3:1, 4:14) Borrowing language from Jewish religious ritual, the author of Hebrews argues that Jesus is the efficacious high priest, even "the great high priest," replacing the temple's high priest, who, as the primary teacher of the Torah, offered a daily sacrifice for the sins of the people. This figure of speech being applied to Christ assumes a readership that is familiar with the priestly tasks of the Jewish temple.

pioneer (Heb 12:2) Alternatively translated as author or leader, this noun carries the dictionary definition of one who opens up new land or venture for others. Sadly, for some Americans, "pioneer" recalls only a national history in which easterners walked across the continent to claim land for themselves, both improving their own situation and destroying that of the native peoples.

sacrifice (1 John 2:2) Continuing the hermeneutic of the fourth evangelist, the author of 1 John states that it is not that Jesus offers a sacrifice but that he is the sacrifice. This imagery speaks especially to the mixed population of the Roman Empire, in which temples and regular animal sacrifices by both pagans and Jews were a normal and expected aspect of daily life, thus making a comparison to Jesus's execution understandable. But even in Psalm 50:14 the Israelites enlarged the word away from its literal meaning and toward a description of personal ethical behavior. Contemporary theologians debate to what degree the historic language of Jesus as a sacrifice ought to remain a dominant figure of speech for the Second Person, with some maintaining that sacrifice is a fundamental requirement of Christian ethics, and others wary about an archaic category that gets commandeered to criticize others' level of devotion. ***Question:*** *How was an execution a sacrifice?*

alpha and omega (Rev 22:13) The first and last letters of the Greek alphabet, used in Revelation 1:8 as a figure of speech for the First Person, become a figure of speech for the eternal and everlasting Second Person of the Godhead, the beginning and end of all things.

rider of the white horse (Rev 19:11) In the apocalyptic visions of the end time, an avenging rider on a white horse is named Faithful and True, the Word of God, King of kings and Lord of lords. For those Christians now and throughout history who have suffered oppression under tyrants, the arrival of such a figure is good news, promising vindication and justice.

root of David (Rev 22:16) The idea that the Messiah would be a descendant of King David, and thus the apex of the monarchical tree, is here reversed, by saying that Jesus is the source of authority that preceded David. The Davidic origin of Christ is expressed also as "the branch of Jesse" and "the tree of Jesse." Many church buildings display a tree of Jesse, in which Jesse reclines in sleep, and from his belly grows an enormous tree, on which appear the biblical ancestors of Jesus.

morning star (Rev 22:16) In antiquity, the planet Venus, which appeared in the east before sunrise, was seen as heralding the coming of day. So as a figure of speech for Christ it claims him as before the beginning. Christians know this figure mostly through Philipp Nicolai's 1597 masterpiece "O Morning Star."[17]

Figures of Speech from the Animal World

Christians were remarkably creative in utilizing real or mythical animals as figures of speech for the Second Person of the Trinity. The preeminent theologian Augustine even asserted that animals could work well as Christological symbols even if the descriptions concerning the animals were not accurate.[18] Here is a short listing of such figures.[19]

butterfly Many Christians are familiar with the depiction of the butterfly as an image for the resurrected Christ, who emerges from the chrysalis of the tomb on Easter. See for example the use of the butterfly in popular digital Easter cards. In the fifth century, Pope Gelasius I likened Christ also to the worm that we call a caterpillar, that became transformed in the resurrection.

eagle Because the eagle long functioned as a symbol of divine power and, among pagans, as the conductor of souls to heaven, it has been used to signify the Second Person. The splendor of the eagle's flight, along with its extraordinary sight and its fierce talons, make it the most powerful predator in the sky. Exegetes in the early church cited Jeremiah 49:22 as substantiation for this image: "He shall mount up and swoop down like an eagle."

fish Perhaps the most well-known of the animal imagery for Christ is the fish, which in our time is either honored or ridiculed by bumper stickers. Because the Greek noun for fish, *ichthus*, happens to be an acrostic for the phrase "Jesus Christ, God's Son, Savior," a depiction of a fish spread throughout the Mediterranean world as a symbol, perhaps a secret one, of Christian faith. In the second century, Tertullian wrote, "We small fish, like our Fish, Jesus Christ, swim in the baptismal water, and we can be saved only by remaining in it."[20] A Trinitarian variation on the fish is the medieval Trinacria, a depiction of three fish fanning out from a single head, and in some artistic depictions of the Last Supper, there is a great fish served on the platter.[21]

lion Although usually used as a symbol of the evangelist Mark, the lion has functioned also as a figure of speech for the Second Person. That it was believed that lions slept with their eyes open led to a comparison with Christ who even in the tomb maintained his divine nature. That it was believed that cubs were stillborn but came to life thanks to the breath of the father on the third day encouraged a comparison with

Christ's resurrection. ***Question:*** *Should all Christian children read C. S. Lewis's The Lion, the Witch and the Wardrobe?*[22]

peacock For centuries, the spectacular beauty of the peacock's tail made it a symbol of immortality and thus for Christians an image for the immortality of Jesus Christ. The peacock appears in several places in the catacombs as a sign of eternal life in Christ.

pelican Because of two mistaken notions about the pelican—that the mother pierced her own breast to feed her young with her blood and that the pelican disappeared for half of the year—much Christian iconography depicted the pelican and her brood as an image of Christ nurturing the baptized.

> *From Thomas Aquinas, in his thirteenth-century hymn* Adore te devote*:*
>
> Thou, like a pelican to feed her brood,
> Didst pierce Thyself to give us living food:
> Thy blood, O Lord, one drop has power to win
> Forgiveness for our world and all its sin.[23]

phoenix Ancient art in both Egypt and China depicted the mythical bird of the phoenix, perhaps modeled on the actual golden pheasant. The legend claimed that the phoenix was born from the sun, without a father or a mother; after a life of five hundred years, it burned itself to death; and it is reborn from its own ashes into a new life. Christians used this myth to illustrate the doctrine of Christ's death and resurrection.

scapegoat Leviticus 16:20–22 describes an annual Israelite Day of Atonement that included a ritual in which the sins of the community were transferred onto a goat which was then released into the wilderness. Some Christians used the scapegoat as a figure of speech for Christ who bears our sins away and releases us from guilt, thus restoring the community.

> *From Pastor Aaron Koch, in a sermon dated March 6, 2022:*
>
> Though Jesus was without sin, yet Jesus submitted to John's baptism, standing shoulder to shoulder with sinners, that He might be our substitute and stand-in. There in the water God the Father made Jesus the scapegoat, laying on His head the guilt of the world, which He would take and carry away.[24]

swallow That the swallow returns each spring became a figure of speech for the resurrection.

swan The white swan figured in many ancient myths. One detail common to these legends was that the swan sang a beautiful death song, which some Christian exegetes set parallel to the final discourse in John 14–17. Christian use of the divine swan of heaven unfortunately stressed the creature's whiteness as a necessary identification with Christ. ***Question:*** *When is Christian use of "white" a worrisome hidden reference to skin color?*

unicorn This mythical beast, resembling a horse with a long single frontal horn, became a popular symbol of Christ during medieval times, especially given the legend that the unique unicorn was tamed by a virgin. Thus, according to William of Normandy, a thirteenth-century author of a Bestiary, "Jesus Christ our Savior is the spiritual unicorn, who made his dwelling in the Virgin."[25] For centuries, the horn of the narwhal, popularly identified as the unicorn's horn, was valued as a nearly magical remedy for many conditions. In about 1500, two renowned sets of tapestries that feature the unicorn were crafted, one now in the Cloisters of the Metropolitan Museum of Art and the other in the Museum of Cluny in Paris. The Resurrection Lutheran Church in Arlington, Virginia, in a Trinitarian sculpture on its building's facade, presents the Second Person as a unicorn.

> *From Jim Cotter's twenty-four "O Antiphons," in the twenty-first century:*
>
> O come, O come, thou unicorn
> appearing in our dreams, lovelorn,
> expectant, quiv'ring, innocent,
> wild messenger with God's intent.
> Rejoice! Rejoice! The Spirit shy
> shall come this night with new-born cry.[26]

Figures of Speech from Christians Past and Present

"Jesus is my air Plane." This is one of my favorites. Go online to view the 1970 art by Sister Gertrude Morgan.[27]

From Niceta of Remesiana in the fifth century:

If you are stumbling, fix your foot firmly on him, for he is a rock: and like a wall he will protect you.[28]

amor meus[29] Let this short quotation echo the many female and male mystics who, especially in the twelfth through the fifteenth centuries, asserted that they were married to Christ. One of the most theologically renowned was Catherine of Siena, while one of the more hyperbolic was Margery Kempe. Margery lived in England from 1373–1440 and, since she claimed to be married to Christ, she negotiated a sexual divorce from her husband and spent her years on pilgrimages to holy places. She was celebrated for her hysterics when contemplating Christ's passion and for her outspoken criticism of the clergy. Illiterate, she dictated her memoirs, which make for lively reading. She claimed that *amor meus* was engraved on the wedding ring that Christ gave her. Both female and male mystics spoke of the experience of mystical marriage.[30] Echoes of it remain in Johann Franck's classic hymn "Soul, Adorn Yourself with Gladness."[31]

From Jacopone da Todi in the thirteenth century:

Love, Love, O Love, thy touch so quickens me. . .
Love, Love, my Love, O take me in a sigh!
Love, glad and spent I lie.
O Love, my Bliss,
O Lover's Kiss!
I quench my soul in Love![32]

apple tree[33] A beloved anonymous eighteenth-century carol praises Christ as an apple tree, laden with fruit, always green, providing shade, a tree that keeps one's faith alive. "His beauty doth all things excel."

athlete[34] In narrating the second-century martyrdoms of Lyon, the church historian Eusebius called Christ "the mighty and conquering Athlete." A tradition developed of describing Christ preparing for death as like the athlete readying for Roman competitions. Perhaps some people far more interested in sports than I am can find this figure of speech helpful.

From "The Dream of the Rood," translated from the eighth-century Old English, in which the cross itself is describing the crucifixion:

I did not dare to break or bow down against the Lord's word,
when I saw the ends of the earth tremble. . . .
Then the young hero made ready—that was God almighty—
strong and resolute; he ascended on the high gallows,
brave in the sight of many, when he wanted to ransom mankind.[35]

bridge[36] In the fourteenth century, Catherine of Siena described at length how Christ is the bridge reaching from heaven to earth, "joining the most high with the most lowly." If not the image itself, at least her development of the image includes both the divine and the human in Christ.

captain[37] "Captain" feels to me, what it is: a seventeenth-century naval figure of speech for Jesus who rescues us from storm and "grave perils," directing the ship of salvation to safety.

carpenter[38] The twentieth-century hymnwriter Richard Leach developed the biographical description in Mark 6:3 of Jesus being a carpenter into an extended figure of speech, in which the tools and tasks of a carpenter are contrasted with the work of the "Savior, Mary's son." The text is thus able to move from the human in Jesus to the divine.

celestial milk[39] From the early third century we have a Hymn to Christ the Savior that is filled with biblical imagery, among which Jesus Christ is named the "celestial Milk out-pressed from a young bride's fragrant breasts." Our culture speaks freely about the sexual attraction of breasts but less about their nutritional use. ***Question:*** *Should we revive this image?*

clothing "He is our clothing, that, for love, wrappeth us up and windeth us about," wrote Julian of Norwich.[40] Enclosed for decades in late medieval England in a hut attached to a church, she claimed that Christ is the clothing she needs. We wear Christ.

constant surprise[41] A favored image of the hymnwriter Herbert Brokering, "surprise" in this Easter hymn written in 1995 describes Jesus at the meal at Emmaus. A surprise occurs in an instant, but the surprise appearance of the risen Christ is constant. Perhaps speaking of the Second Person always suggests using an oxymoron.

crown In the current English translation of Philipp Nicolai's *Wie schön leuchtet*, the Lord Jesus is called "crown of gladness."[42] I think of the crown placed on the head of King Charles III. I think of the crown of flowers that both a bride and a groom wore for their wedding. I think of how one feels upon receiving a great honor. "O Morning Star" calls Jesus our crown, the marvelous marker of an extraordinary transformation of the self into something more and other than it was.

dayspring[43] Meant to be sung on December 21, the date observing the winter solstice in the northern hemisphere, this stanza of "O Come, O Come, Emmanuel" is a translation from the sixth-century "O Antiphons," which were sung as Magnificat antiphons on the seven days preceding Christmas. The Latin for the daystar, the rising sun, was "Oriens."

eternal victim[44] In his 1745 hymn "O thou Eternal Victim slain," Charles Wesley enlarged the traditional imagery of the crucified Christ as a victim, whether of God's wrath or of imperial injustice, with the adjective "eternal," thus granting to Golgotha in the first century everlasting import. In a collect for Good Friday, Janet Morley calls Christ "our victim."[45] ***Question:*** *Does this suggest a victim for us? by us? belonging to us?*

everlasting instant[46] In "You, Lord, Are Both Lamb and Shepherd," twentieth-century hymnwriter Sylvia Dunstan sets each figure of speech next to its opposite: lamb and shepherd, prince and slave, peacemaker and sword-bringer. Each stanza concludes with the oxymoron "everlasting instant": in this phrase, even time must bend to the mystery of Christ.

feast[47] First published in 1633 and then cast as a hymn in 1908, George Herbert's poem "Come, my way, my truth, my life" presents nine biblical images for Christ. "My feast" recalls John 2 and the wedding of Cana. Incongruously, Christians commonly refer to the bite of bread and the swallow of wine of the eucharist as a banquet and feast.

gardener[48] In 1966 Fred Kann wrote "We meet you, O Christ," celebrating the many guises in which we encounter the Second Person. Here, Mary Magdalene's mistake in thinking that the risen Christ was a gardener becomes a figure of speech to laud Christ, "a tree on your back." When each week at worship our intercessions pray for the well-being of the earth, we might call Christ our gardener.

hiding place[49] Along with John Newton's 1779 hymn "How Sweet the Name of Jesus Sounds," all eight stanzas of Jehoiada Brewer's 1776 hymn "Hail, Sovereign Love," apparently a treasured text given that it was included in 221 hymnals, concluded with the figure that Jesus is our hiding place. ***Question:*** *From what do we need to hide?*

jewel[50] "for him all stars have shown," wrote the twentieth-century poet Elizabeth Jennings in "A Christmas Sequence." We adorn ourselves with Christ, this jewel "of untold worth."

key of David[51] The sixth-century "O Antiphons" assign this Christological figure of speech for use on December 20. Inspired by Isaiah 22:22, this figure imagines the coming one as the major domo who has authority over the keeping of the household. In Revelation 3:7, Christ holds the key; in much Christian iconography, Peter is holding the keys to heaven; but in the "O Antiphons," Christ is the key.

knight[52] Recently used as a title of a book, the first known use of a knight in shining armor as an image for Christ is in an anonymous 1215 text *Ancrene Riwle*, in which the knight Christ dies while saving the maiden in distress. I doubt that in the twenty-first century we can take this figure of speech seriously.

leader of the dance[53] Worshipers might guess that this figure of speech arose in the 1960s, but it was during the first few generations of the church that Christ was named as the leader of the dance.

lily of the valley[54] The self-taught Charles A. Tindley, the son of an enslaved African American, became a Methodist minister and composer of many gospel songs. "When the Storms of Life are Raging," written in 1906, uses the image in the Song of Songs 2:2, in which the male lover is likened to a lily of the valley. In the second century, the biblical scholar Origen interpreted the "valley" as the world and the "lily" as Christ. During Tindley's lifetime, the lily of the valley symbolized immortality.

manna John Newton, the eighteenth-century author of "Amazing Grace," wrote "How Sweet the Name of Jesus Sounds," a hymn that with five verbs and fifteen nouns is itself a thesaurus of figures of speech for the Second Person. Toward the conclusion, Newton wrote, "But when I see thee as thou art, I'll praise thee as I ought." In the meantime, we can sing hymns such as his. "Manna" recalls John 6:31, 49–51.

mighty Lord of armies, gentle Prince of Peace[55] In this 1893 hymn, the militarism of all its battle imagery is softened with a few references to peace and comfort. Many recent hymn collections omit such texts. The question remains whether "Christian soldier" texts are emotionally useful as a strong figure of speech for Christ, or are inappropriate as sanctifying warfare. Here it is Christ who is leading the armies. ***Question:*** *On each June 6, do you watch video clips of the Normandy invasion?*

pearl[56] The seventeenth-century Anglican John Mason cited the pearl of great price from the parable in Matthew 13:46 to open his nine-stanza praise of Christ. Mason's hymn lists thirty-eight figures of speech for Christ. But I fear that it is no longer sung.

> *From John Mason, from "I've found the pearl of great price," in the seventeenth century:*
>
> Christ's manhood is a temple, where
> The altar God doth rest;
> My Christ, he is the sacrifice,
> My Christ, he is the priest.
>
> Christ is my meat, Christ is my drink,
> My physic and my health,
> My peace, my strength, my joy, my crown,
> My glory and my wealth.

ransom[57] A current translation of Martin Luther's hymn "Dear Christians, One and All Rejoice," which literalizes a conversation between God the Father and God the Son concerning the incarnation, cites "ransom," an image used since Mark 10:45: he "gave his life as a ransom for many." As developed especially in the second century, the ransom was the price God had to pay to the devil, in whose power humans were held captive from the Fall until the resurrection. In the fourth century, Gregory of Nazianzus judged this image to be inappropriate for the faith,[58] although it remains an important figure of speech in some spiritualities.

rice[59] The twentieth-century Methodist pastor and missionary Andrew Fowler wrote this hymn in acknowledgment that in many Asian cultures, it is rice, not wheat, that constitutes the staple of life. The hymn includes this line: "The rice of God for all is meant."

rose[60] In the well-known fifteenth-century Christmas carol, the biblical imagery of the tree of Jesse has expanded into praise for the rose blooming on the tree. See Song of Songs 2:1. For Christians, the rose is Christ, "true man, yet very God," says the hymn text.

song[61] In a hymn adopted by the L'Arche Community of homes for adults with disabilities, Jesus is my song, not only when gathered in worship, but wherever I journey. We sing Jesus.

sower and seed[62] In an expert 1998 hymn constructed with a double figure of speech, Herman Stuempfle wrote of the Second Person as the Sower, who cast the seed, who sowed his own life, who as a Seed was buried, who awoke at God's command, and who is now among us as both Sower and Seed. The hymnwriter expanded the usual interpretation of the parable of the sower into an accessible Christological poem.

Beginning in "ancient hills" and concluding in the lives of fruitful Christians, the hymn is a model of creative openness to biblical figures of speech.

stupendous stranger[63] Perhaps during one of his stays in either debtor's prison or in a lunatic asylum (the diagnosis was "religious mania"!), the eighteenth-century poet Christopher Smart wrote "Where is this stupendous Stranger?" The poem gives the answer to this question: this "most Mighty" is found in the manger.

treasure[64] First published in 1653, Johann Franck's German hymn was translated by Catherine Winkworth, who masterfully concluded the final stanza by rhyming "priceless treasure" with "purest pleasure."

tree of life In Judaism, the Torah has been called the "tree of life."[65] In Christianity, as we see in the renowned hymns from the sixth-century poet Venantius Honorius Fortunatus, "Sing, My Tongue," and "The Royal Banners Forward Go," the cross of Christ has been named the beauteous tree.[66] In the seventeenth century, the Hungarian pastor Pécselyi Király Imre composed a lengthy poem on the passion that in the twentieth century the hymnologist Erik Routley shaped into the hymn "There in God's Garden."[67] In this complex poem, the Tree of all that is good is a figure of speech for Christ himself. As the notes in an Orthodox Study Bible state, the tree of life is "a symbol of Christ Himself."[68] Recent hymns by Marty Haugen and by Susan Palo Cherwien have continued this tradition.[69]

From Ann Griffiths in the eighteenth century:

I am yearning for that moment
when my privilege is sure,
where the tree of life, Christ Jesus,
who is justice, whole and pure,
steadfast grace, hiding place,
takes the futile fig-leaves' place![70]

window[71] In a candid poem about the world's injustices, Brian Wren asserts that our faith accompanies us until we see divine justice accomplished. The final stanza names Christ as "our sign, our window into God," who awakens hope and points a way ahead. We see through Christ to God.

Some Second Person Issues to Consider

About Arianism: Christianity has long discussed the issue of how to balance expressions that speak of the human and of the divine in Christ. During the fourth century, as theologians were conferring about how best to articulate their faith in and experience of God as revealed in the Scriptures—how, we might say, to manifest the mystery—a dominant voice in the debates was Arianism. Arianism, in some ways a more accessible theology than what became orthodox Christianity, taught that Christ was a creature secondary to God. God was the Father, whole and one. Christ, similar to the demigods of other religions, was a human born from a divine father and a human mother whose extraordinary exploits brought about salvation for needy humankind. Yet as Hercules was not Zeus, it followed for Arius that it was inappropriate to claim that Christ is equal to and one with the Father. Arius, who clearly was resistant to religious paradox, would not have applauded Martin Luther for such comments as "God feeds the whole world through a Babe nursing at Mary's breast."[72] However, opposition to Arius prevailed. Arianism was condemned as heresy, and the centuries of creativity in expressing the Trinity marked Christian life and witness.

Along with the fourth-century Cappadocian theologians who shaped our speech concerning orthodox Trinitarian doctrine, I judge that we ought to maintain the paradox of the divine and human natures of the Second Person. In an attempt to maintain Trinitarian orthodoxy, the following wording for a Trinitarian benediction has been proposed: "God, the Source of glory, God, the Word of Life, God, the Spirit of truth, bless you all, now and forever."[73] Yet to avoid the binary male language of Father and Son, many contemporary hymns and prayers name the First Person as God and the Second as Jesus. This common current practice obscures the shared divinity within the triune God. ***Question:*** *Is "God, Jesus, and the Spirit" a return to the Arian heresy? If so, does it matter?*

> *From Pope Damasus, in the fourth century:*
>
> Hope, Life, Way, Salvation,
> Understanding, Wisdom, Light,
> Judge, Door, Most High, King,
> Precious Stone, Prophet, Priest,
> Messiah, Sabaoth, Teacher,
> Spouse, Mediator,
> Scepter, Dove, Hand, Stone, Song,
> and Emmanuel,
> Vineyard, Shepherd, Sheep, Peace,
> Root, Vine-stock, Olive Tree,
> Source, Wall, Lamb, Victim,
> Lion, Intercessor,
> Word, Man, Net, Rock, House:
> Christ Jesus is everything.[74]

About Jesus: An opposite problem was commonplace during especially the nineteenth century. God becomes only something of an inexplicable idea, and Christianity becomes only about Jesus, god or godlike, wonder worker, bonded with us in suffering, a great and simple superman narrated in stories too often literalized, albeit penned by evangelists each saying in a distinctive manner that there is more to Jesus than Jesus. ***Question:*** *How does Jesus deal with Trinity, and the Trinity with Jesus?*

About the two natures of Christ: We have seen that some figures of speech listed here stress the divine nature of the Second Person, with more of them in recent centuries elaborating on Christ's human nature. Some authors introduce paradoxes and oxymorons into their text—for example, Charles Wesley's "eternal victim"—to indicate with one expression both the divine and the human. Indeed, one theologian wrote explicitly about the need for paradox to correct analogy when engaging in God-talk.[75] In A. S. Byatt's novel *The Children's Book* is an intriguing articulation of the dual nature of the Second Person: "There are chinks of light, moments of stasis, between one state and another, between the victories of the Pale Galilean and the multiform Life-Force."[76] The Pale Galilean and the multiform Life-Force: a remarkable dual expression.

As with the First Person, many figures of speech that honor the Second Person are not anthropomorphic but rather objective: Christ who is rock, shield, hiding place, treasury, gate, morning star, pelican, clothing, lily of the valley, tree of life. The Second Person is often encountered as not a person but a thing. Always we must remember that when speaking of God, analogy is useful but insufficient, since God is always unlike whatever simile we propose.

Yet at least in the English language, the good news about the anthropomorphisms used for the Second Person is that many are nongendered. The church refers to the Second Person as rabbi, teacher, pioneer, lover, athlete, captain, carpenter, victim, gardener, sower, stranger. Although for an older generation these nouns may still drag along a cultural sense of masculine gender, none of these words is grammatically masculine or feminine in gender, and none need be dealt with as male terms. As well, in prayer and song, the pronoun for direct address is the nongendered "you."[77] We can generally use the (grammatical) second person for the (doctrinal) Second Person. ***Question:*** *How might languages that maintain grammatically gendered nouns escape old-style masculinity?*

> *From Michael Frye, "Jesus, Be the Center," in the twentieth century:*
>
> Jesus, be the center, be my source,
> be my light,
> Jesus.
> Be the fire in my heart.
> Be the wind in these sails.
> Be the reason that I live,
> Jesus.[78]

About the liturgical year: One way to speak as fully as possible about the Second Person is by celebrating as fully as possible the entire liturgical year. The festivals of the incarnation provide one example. In the ecumenical three-year lectionary, there are three different sets of biblical readings that welcome the incarnation. In the appointed texts for Christmas Eve, the first reading, Isaiah 9:2–7, praises the child born for us. The beloved gospel reading is the narrative from Luke 2 of the birth of the infant, even mentioning how the mother Mary clothed the newborn. In the texts appointed for Christmas Day, the first reading from Isaiah 52:7–10 opens with the announcement "Your God reigns," and the gospel reading from John 1 lauds the Son who is the Word, God from before creation, from whom comes all the life of the world. It is to be desired that the chosen hymnody, the choir music, the preaching, and the printed or projected art for Christmas Eve will build upon the image of the infant in the manger, and that for Christmas Day will proclaim the incarnation of the Trinity. The third set, appointed for the Epiphany, holds together the human with the divine by narrating an event in the life of a young child who is welcomed by a cosmic phenomenon and who receives gifts from religious seers that acclaim the child as divine royalty.

In recent decades, by far the largest number of Christians attend worship on Christmas Eve, with Christmas Day spent in family gatherings and without any thought given to John 1, and the smallest number worshiping on Epiphany. It is true that on Christmas Eve, a Christian reading of Isaiah 9 sees that the child is named Mighty God, Everlasting Father, Prince of Peace, Wonderful Counselor—that is, in the child is the triune God. ***Question:*** *Which hymns ought to be sung on Christmas Eve to best unite the human and the divine in the manger?*

The classic liturgy of Good Friday provides another example of the binding into one the two natures of Christ.[79] In an opening prayer, the assembly speaks of the Second Person as "our Lord Jesus Christ," "our Savior and Lord." The first reading (Isa. 52:13–53:12) speaks of the servant, a root out of dry ground, a man of suffering, a lamb, a ewe, and an offering for sin. Psalm 22:1–21 speaks of the one forsaken by God, a worm, one surrounded by strong bulls and packs of dogs, and in verses 22–31 praises the one who rules over the nations. The second reading from Hebrews speaks of the blood of Christ, the curtain of his flesh, a great priest, the Son of God. In the Johannine passion, the arresting police fall to the ground as he speaks the *ego eimi*, the I AM, and the narrative refers to him as the King of the Jews and the Son of God. The bidding prayer addresses all petitions to the First Person "through Christ our Lord." The procession of the cross calls everyone to worship the one who was hung on the life-giving cross. The hymns that are recommended are those that liken the cross to the tree of life. If the worship includes the holy communion, bread and wine are called the body and blood of Christ. We see then that Good Friday, from Isaiah's ewe to the Johannine I AM, is itself a thesaurus for the Second Person of the Trinity.

As with the First Person, so with the Second: figures of speech for God are a challenge for us human speakers. But enriching the language of communal worship with classic and innovative figures of speech might help.

5

THE THIRD PERSON, FIGURATIVELY SPEAKING

The Third Person: Who, What, How

CHRISTIAN THEOLOGY HAS taught that coequal with the First and the Second Persons of the Trinity is the Third, who logically would receive one-third of Christian focus and devotion. While the Azusa Street revival of 1906 and the celebrative enthusiasm in Pentecostal worship are examples of an explosive rise of invocation of and praise to the Spirit in the early twentieth century, it remains the case that in some spiritualities, and characteristically in the Western liturgical tradition, this Spirit is seldom directly addressed, except perhaps on Pentecost and at rituals of ecclesial blessing. Rather, the First Person is asked to send the Third. Perhaps this accounts for the fact that many figures of speech for the Third Person are objective, as if this Person is a thing to be sent, likened to an object in nature, rather than being anthropomorphic, understood as a person-like phenomenon, engaging in personal interaction.

In the Eastern church, it is the Father who sends the Spirit, and in the West, it is the Father and the Son who send the Spirit. The fourth Gospel can be cited in support of each position. This ostensibly arcane difference has more meaning in the present and future than it might have had in the past. Since many Christians are praying more often now for the Spirit of God to come onto persons who are not Christian, it may be that the controversial phrase in the Nicene creed, "and the Son," gets in some people's way. There are indeed some Western Christians who advocate that the Nicene creed as spoken in the West ought to return to its original fourth-century text, by omitting the sixth-century addition of "Filioque." Yet this theological conversation appears not to impinge upon the figures of speech that worldwide Christians utilize: the East and the West currently use similar figures of speech for the Third Person. ***Question:*** *Should "and the Son" be removed from the Western text of the Nicene creed?*

From Delores Dufner OSB, "O Spirit All-Embracing," in the twenty-first century:

O Spirit all-embracing and counselor all-wise,
unbounded splendor gracing a shoreless sea of skies . . .
Come, stream of endless flowing. . .
come, wind of springtime blowing . . .
O Beauty ever blazing in flower, field, and face. . .
Come fire of glory gracious. . .
undying flame tenacious, burn in your church anew.[1]

A second historical controversy concerns access to this Third Person: is such availability granted to the church in assembly, or to the individual in prayer? That is, is the Third Person promised to the ecclesial institution formed through baptism, or does this power come also, or even mainly, to the charismatic individual outside of the sanction of church leadership? Later in this chapter is cited the remarkable invocation of the Spirit written in the tenth century by the monk Symeon. The Eastern Church granted to Symeon the honorific "the New Theologian" in recognition of his claim that, like the biblical evangelists who personally experienced the vision of God and thus were qualified to be named as theologians, an individual believer could receive God in episodes of private and unique ecstasy. Although the charismatic movement is often traced back to the Azusa Street revival in Los Angeles, it may be more accurate to see Symeon's somewhat idiosyncratic writings about the Holy Spirit as an ur-foundation of Pentecostalism. Far from the remark in Acts 19:2, that the Christians in Ephesus are quoted as saying "We have not even heard that there is a Holy Spirit," charismatic Christians tend to place the Spirit front and center in the Trinity. Yet also this theological conversation appears not to impinge upon the figures of speech that worldwide Christians utilize: the worshiping assembly and the ecstatic individual share similar figures of speech for the Third Person. ***Question:*** *In English, must the word "spirit" be capitalized if the Third Person of the Trinity is intended?*

There is, however, a theological conversation that does influence our figures of speech, and that is the matter of divine gender. Before we list and discuss figures of speech that invoke or describe the Third Person using gendered categories, we might here review the current controversial situation concerning gender in Christian theology and in American English.

Historic Christian theology has maintained that God has no sex. That is, God is literally neither male nor female. While some Christians regularize or even mandate male language for God, most teach that all anthropomorphic language to and about God, except when dealing with the incarnation of God in Jesus, must be understood as metaphoric figurative speech, and such speech can become problematic if literalized.[2] But Christians in some cultures now face the question whether their religious language ought to grant God, if not sex, then gender. In essentialist thinking, biological sex ought to determine cultural gendered life. Thus to be a male or female ought by nature to result in certain human predispositions, and according to the essentialist, these are to be expressed in cultural gender.

Some Christians are glad to extend essentialist thinking to language for God. Thus even though God has no sex, there would be some meaning in the language that God, who has the natural power and authority to rule, might be appropriately granted masculine gender. In the early centuries of the church, especially some Eastern writers, more often than in the West, applied this essentialist thinking when it referred to the nurturing Third Person as feminine. In our time, some Christians who lean toward essentialism find it appropriate, if not mandated, to call the First Person "he," and to allow, if not to encourage, the Third Person to be "she." "It" is rejected, as dismissive of the personal relationship between God and the believer. "They" would be problematic, since despite its recent usage as a singular personal pronoun, it introduces the memory of polytheism into Christian speech. ***Question:*** *Is it helpful to think of God as intersex?*

> *From the* Hudra *of the Church of the East during Epiphany, fifth century:*
>
> The Holy Spirit was sent,
> she overshadowed the baptismal font
> and in the womb of the water, in
> the "Jordan,"
> she fashioned infants who will not die,
> and they became spiritual bridegrooms
> in whom there dwells Christ the King.[3]

Yet increasingly in American thought, essentialist thinking is being challenged, with gender understood as fluid.[4] According to this thinking, gender is not God-given but a socially constructed proposal for thought and practice. We have become aware that across the globe and throughout history various cultures assign gender in quite different ways, and thus the notion that personality inclinations or communal responsibilities are determined by physical sexuality is inaccurate. Furthermore, persons are now able to alter their own sexual characteristics and their gender designation and to choose for themselves their preferred pronoun. To the extent that this view becomes the norm, calling the First Person "he" and the Third Person "she" is theologically misgendering and introduces essentialist static into contemporary Christian speech. But some recent denominational hymn collections boldly go where few men have gone before, to refer to especially the Third Person as "she," and this chapter will give examples of this practice.

While the ecumenical movement has lessened the theological and cultural distinctions among the denominations that have arisen over the past five hundred years, it may be that future divisions within the worldwide church will reflect opposite answers to the questions of literalization. Is the Spirit literally a She? Is God somehow literally Father? Was there a factual virgin birth? Is there literally a personal life after death? Should Christians utilize only close translations of biblical speech, while others judge that an inspired church will add new figures of speech to its vocabulary? Perhaps we already are witnessing that, rather than fight these issues out, Christians are finding it expedient to meet in different buildings for Sunday worship. ***Question:*** *How does the Third Person want to be referred to, as he? she? it?*

This chapter will now consider many figures of speech for the Third Person, first those found in the Bible, then in the ninth-century *Veni Creator Spiritus*, in the twelfth-century *Veni Sancte Spiritus*, then in the work of Symeon the New Theologian, and finally from other Christians past and present.

Figures of Speech from the Scriptures

ruah (Gen. 1:2) In the opening sentences of the Bible we encounter the fascinating Hebrew word *ruah*. Each of its possible translations has been used by Christians as figures of speech for the Third Person of the Trinity. The word "spirit" suggests an animating principle of life; an unseen yet powerful force; an energy transmitted and shared beyond itself. For some Christians, the ambiguity of Spirit is an advantage for religious speech. To distinguish God's Spirit from many other possible spirits, Christians have affixed the adjective "Holy," and in English have capitalized Spirit.

> *From Doris Akers, "Sweet, Sweet Spirit," in the twentieth century:*
>
> There's a sweet, sweet Spirit in this place,
> and I know that it's the Spirit of the Lord.
> Sweet Heavenly Dove, stay right here with us,
> filling us with your love.[5]

In Hebrew, *ruah* also means wind, and many contemporary Bibles use this word in rendering Genesis 1:2. Wind is a force of nature that we cannot see, blowing where it will (John 3:8), although we see its many effects around us. It can nurture, it can destroy. The recent hymn "Spirit of Gentleness" features wind as the primary image of the Spirit, as its refrain reads "Spirit of restlessness, stir me from placidness, wind, wind on the sea."[6] Meanwhile, the hymn "God of Tempest, God of Whirlwind" speaks of the mighty and wild power of God as wind.[7] It may be that especially ecologically minded Christians appreciate this connection of the energy of God with an uncontrolled force of nature.

In Hebrew, *ruah* also means breath. "Breath" is commonly used in rendering Genesis 6:17 and is well-known in the vision of the dry bones in Ezekiel 37. Recently one Christian has suggested that the Breath of God is a helpful way to speak of the Third Person of the Trinity, God being the Father, the Son, and the Breath of the Father into the Son.[8] In the past, it was common for the ritual of baptism to include the presider breathing into the face of the initiate, although in our time concerns about contagion have deleted this gesture. It may be that breath as a figure of speech for the Third Person may provide the faithful a reasonable use of anthropomorphism.

> *From Osvaldo Catena, translated by Gerhard Cartford, "O living Breath of God," in the twentieth century:*
>
> O living Breath of God, wind at the
> beginning upon the waters;
> O living Breath of God, bearing the
> creation to wondrous birth:
> Come now, and fill our spirits; pour
> out your gifts abundant.
> O living Breath of God, Holy Spirit,
> breathe in us as we pray.[9]

Finally, and for some Christians first, in Hebrew, *ruah* is a noun of feminine gender. Some languages assign all nouns a grammatical gender—either female, male, or neuter. Oftentimes the grammatical gender has no relationship with the actual purported sex of what the noun is naming: for example, in German, *mädchen*, meaning girl, is grammatically neuter. The language Anglo-Saxon had grammatical gender, glimpsed only rarely in modern English when, for example, a country, a ship, or the church is a "she." Currently there is contemporary interest in this linguistic memory of a feminine "Spirit," and there are calls for a return to this historic practice by its adoption by even English-speaking Christians.

dove (Mark 1:10) Perhaps the evangelist intended that the dove appearing to Jesus at his baptism meant to recall the dove signaling peace at the conclusion of the flood in Genesis 8:11. Baptismal texts and ecclesial art have made much of this dove, in white flight above the assembly and descending as the blessing of God.

> *From T. S. Eliot, in "Little Gidding," in the twentieth century:*
>
> The dove descending breaks the air
> With flame of incandescent terror
> Of which the tongues declare
> The one discharge from sin and error. . .[10]

power of the Most High (Luke 1:35) In the Lucan narrative of the annunciation to Mary, the "Holy Spirit" and "the power of the Most High" are synonyms. Some recent doxologies have used "the Power of the Most High" as the designation for the Third Person.[11] Christians may appreciate the force that "power" gives to a gentle wind or a dove of peace.

finger of God (Luke 11:20) Some Christians have taken this phrase in Luke as a designation for the Holy Spirit, by whose power Jesus casts out demons. Like breath, it offers some anthropomorphism to the amorphous Third Person.

rivers of living water (John 7:37–39) This episode in the Gospel according to John situates Jesus at the Jewish religious ritual during which water was poured on the altar in the temple. As we have come to expect, the fourth Gospel transfers the source of many images to Christ: thus here, the water from the pool of Siloam leads to Jesus himself. Verse 39 works to clarify this source with a reference to the Spirit. Thus Ambrose and others of the church fathers used this passage as a figure of the speech for the Third Person.[12] Christians can think of all the rivers and lakes and pools and fonts filled with flowing life of the Third Person for baptism.

advocate (John 14:16) In the final chapters of the Gospel according to John, the Greek *paraklētos* is a significant designation for the Third Person. With an original first-century usage of defense attorney, this difficult noun is variously rendered in current Bible translations as advocate, counselor, companion, comforter, friend, helper, and heavenly intercessor. It is as if, standing before God, we require the assistance of one who is divine, and in Christian tradition, this one is the Third Person. ***Question:*** *Which is your preferred English rendering of paraklētos?*

seal (2 Cor 1:22) In this passage, seal and Spirit can be seen as synonyms. In antiquity, a seal certified authenticity or identified ownership, and Christian descriptions of chrismation speak of the seal as the presence of the Spirit. We still speak of an envelope being sealed, and perhaps this standard usage can give meaning to this figure of speech for the Third Person.

lord (2 Cor 3:17) "Now the Lord is the Spirit," writes Paul, and Christians repeat this language in the Nicene Creed.

truth (1 John 5:6) Perhaps the word *truth* here can be seen as more than an abstract noun, but as the most profound and solid reality by which the world functions.

The following are figures of speech in the ninth-century hymn *Veni Creator Spiritus*, attributed to Rabanus Maurus:[13]

creator That this classic hymn calls the Third Person, rather than the First Person, creator, is an indication of the theological problem of assigning specific tasks to each member of the Trinity. Eighteenth-century deism maintained that creation was a single event of God in the far distant past, but Christians believe that the triune Creator continues creation daily, throughout the universe and in each living self. ***Question:*** *What should we do about the countless hymns that call the First Person the creator?*

comforter In the past, "comforter" was a primary designation for the Third Person. Since in current usage a comforter is an especially warm blanket, one wonders whether this figure of speech for God is still effective.

gift of God This figure of speech fits well with the traditional idea that the Spirit is a blessing given from God to the faithful.

fount of life One hopes that for Christians the baptismal reference is clear.

fire of love As we saw in chapter 2, the figure of speech of God being fire was more common in the past than in the present. Here the natural phenomenon of fire has been mitigated, perhaps even erased, by the presence of divine love.

> *From Victoria Walton, in the twentieth century:*
>
> O flaming Spirit of love,
> we cry to you in the midst of the struggles of
> our lives!
> O sacred fire, empower us! . . .
> O God of fire,
> burn within us,
> heal us, strengthen us,
> remake us,
> empower us with your passion for justice![14]

anointing oil In antiquity, oil was prized as restoring well-being to dry limbs and desiccated skin. Early Christian treatises concerning baptism made the ritual of anointing a preeminent sign of the Spirit, with the newly oiled Christian likened to a Greek athlete prepared for competition. The Eastern churches have maintained the significance of chrismation as constitutive in baptism, and some Orthodox Christians question the legitimacy of baptisms that do not include the anointing with oil. ***Question:*** *Should our congregations do more with anointing the initiate at baptism?*

guide For many contemporary believers who think of their lives as a journey, the figure of speech that the Third Person is guide is significant.

Figures of speech in the twelfth-century hymn *Veni Sancte Spiritus*, attributed to Stephen Langton, follow.[15] Along with its many verbs, here are some of the nouns invoked:

father of the poor *Pater pauperum* says the Latin, although most contemporary translations alter this figure of speech. Here the Third Person is titled Father, as is common with the First, except that the patriarchal title is clarified by the inclusion of "the poor," a wake-up call to those of us who are not poor. ***Question:*** *Does the addition of "the poor" strengthen or diminish the figure of Father?*

source In several places in the New Testament (Heb 2:4, 1 Cor 12:4), the Third Person is the source of gifts given to the faithful, which gifts are then to be shared within the community (Rom 12:6). In contrast, Matthew 7:11 identifies the giver of gifts as the Father, and Ephesians 4:11 the giver is Christ. Dividing up divine tasks among the Persons of the Trinity is perhaps not a helpful way forward.

light Traditionally, it was light, not darkness, that was identified with the Godhead, and in a world prior to artificial sources of illumination, it was both natural and logical to assume that there could be no human life without divine light.

consoler That the Third Person comforts those who suffer supports believers in the faith when it appears that, although we ask, God is not providing health and well-being.

guest That the Third Person of God is a guest in the self, not a permanent resident, contrasts with a primary tenet of

Quakerism, an idea that has become widely accepted in our time, that God is by nature in each individual inner self.

rest We can recall the treasured words of Augustine in the first paragraph of his *Confessions*: You have made us for yourself, and our hearts are restless until they rest in you.

Figures of speech in the "Mystical Prayer" of the tenth-century Symeon the New Theologian:

Come, true light.
Come, eternal life.
Come, hidden mystery.
Come, nameless treasure.
Come, ineffable reality.
Come, inconceivable person.
Come, endless bliss.
Come, non-setting sun.
Come, infallible expectation of all those who must be saved.
Come, awakening of those who are asleep.
Come, resurrection of the dead.
Come, O Powerful One.
Come, O invisible and totally intangible and impalpable. . . .
Come, O beloved Name and repeated everywhere. . .
Come, eternal joy.
Come, non-tarnishing crown.
Come, purple of the great king our God.
Come, crystalline cincture, studded with precious stones.
Come, inaccessible sandal.

Come, sovereign right hand.
Come, You the Lonely. . . .
Come, the absolutely inaccessible one.
Come, my breath and my life.
Come, consolation of my poor soul.
Come, my joy, my glory, my endless delight.[16]

***Question:** Which is your favorite line in this invocation?*

Figures of Speech for the Third Person from Other Christians Past and Present

armor Aware of the assaults of evil that may come her way, "armor of the heart" is a figure of speech for the Third Person in Hildegard of Bingen's "Sequence for the Holy Spirit."[17] The addition of "of the heart" alters our image of "armor."

> *From Merlin Robert Carothers, in the twentieth century:*
>
> I realized that Satan and the Spirit of Christ were at war. The pain reached an overwhelming state; I held on to thoughts of praise and thanks and suddenly I was being flooded with joy.[18]

artist[19] The hymnwriter Ruth Duck encourages the church to artistic expression of all kinds in worship, and she invokes the Great Artist of creation to assist us. Choosing art for Christian adornment or for lectionary elaboration is fraught with various difficulties, and so it is a mercy that the Third Person can assist our deliberations.

balm The early twentieth-century African American spiritual "There is a balm in Gilead" gives a Christian answer to the question in Jeremiah 8:22: yes, there is a balm, and it is the Holy Spirit who revives my soul.[20]

captain[21] Usually applied to the Second Person of the Trinity, "captain" is one of the many figures of speech used by Catherine of Siena when she wrote that the church is a ship, captained by the Spirit.

cleanser In Jean Janzen's hymnic version of the writings of Hildegard of Bingen, Janzen calls the Holy Spirit "the cleanser of all things."[22] As I sing this line, I think of old advertisements of a woman scrubbing away to scour the sink: a thought-provoking figure of speech for the Third Person.

cloud Repeatedly in the Bible, God arrives as a cloud or in a cloud. A cloud leads the Israelites on their journey; a cloud fills the temple in Jerusalem with God's presence; at the transfiguration of Jesus, a voice comes from a cloud; in Acts 1:9, a cloud takes Jesus away from the disciples' sight. So it is not surprising that Charles Wesley describes the Spirit as "the cloud of your protecting love."[23]

current of power[24] In "O Fiery Spirit," her adaptation of the writings of Hildegard of Bingen, Jody L. Caldwell calls the Third Person "current of power." The theologian Jurgen Moltmann employs terms like energy, power, and force-field to describe the Spirit.[25] Such figures of speech mean to enliven our sense of the activity of the Third Person. ***Question:*** *Do they?*

> *From John B. Geyer, "We Know That Christ Is Raised," in the twentieth century:*
>
> The Spirit's fission shakes the church of God.
> Baptized, we live with God the Three-in-One.[26]

delight In one of her hymns Madeleine Forell Marshall calls the Third Person "sweet delight."[27] There is a lightness to this figure of speech, a surprise tone amid the heavier images to which we are accustomed.

dew[28] Some Christians have applied the biblical imagery of dew as a figure of speech for the Third Person. In the seventh stanza of "O Holy Ghost, Descend We Pray," Michael Schirmer invoked the "gentle dew" of the Holy Ghost. Urban Christians may be quite unfamiliar with the indispensable natural phenomenon of dew.

frame[29] Written for the 1991 assembly of the World Council of Churches, the text of "Spirit of Love" elaborates on the imagery of weaving. The Third Person is called the frame on which history, like a great loom, is woven.

friend and lover[30] Shirley Erena Murray likens the "loving Spirit" to a mother and a father, and she calls the Spirit friend and lover. In recent decades, the noun "friend" has been commandeered by social media to designate any addressee, while "lover" still retains its twentieth-century connotation of sexual partner. Thus it is that even simple nouns may bring with them complex connotations of meaning.

From Tom Colvin, "God Sends Us His Spirit," in the twentieth century:

Spirit of our Maker, Spirit-Friend.
Spirit of our Jesus, Spirit-Friend.
Spirit of God's people, Spirit-Friend.[31]

ghost In Anglo-Saxon, the language of England before the eleventh century, *gast* was the translation of the Latin *spiritus* and meant "an animating principle." Although in the fourteenth century, "ghost" came to refer to the soul of a dead person, it took over half a millennium, until the second half of the twentieth century, for churches to replace "Ghost" with "Spirit," and we might still encounter Ghost in texts at worship. Let this be an example to us of the conservative nature of liturgical language.

hand of God In recent times, some Christians have spoken about "the right hand" of God as blessing and "the left hand" as punishment. But in the second century Bishop Irenaeus wrote of the right and left hands of God as the Son and the Holy Spirit.[32] According to this figure of speech, the Second and Third Persons are the instruments of the First, the power that do the will of the Godhead.

healer[33] Marty Haugen's hymn "Healer of our every ill," was composed in 1986 at the mountain retreat center Holden Village, in memorial of those who died in the crash of the space shuttle the Challenger. "Our every ill" includes death, destruction, and disappointment. The hymn calls the Third Person the Spirit of all comfort, of all kindness, of compassion.

helper[34] Toyohiko Kagawa (1888–1960) was an extraordinary Japanese layman who, although experiencing considerable societal rejection, dedicated his life to advocating for the poor, improving the lives of oppressed women, establishing hospitals, and promoting pacifism. The Holy Spirit, he wrote, was his helper, so that he could help others.

key "She is the key opening the scriptures," sings the Iona community in a hymn by John L. Bell and Graham Maule. The hymn includes other starting figures of speech for the Third Person, including the "enemy of apathy."[35] One version of the confession of sin for Ash Wednesday lists "pride, envy, hypocrisy, and apathy that have infected our lives."[36] ***Question:*** *Would your assembly agree that apathy is an evil?*

From "She Sits Like a Bird," by John Bell and Graham Maule, in the twentieth century:

She sits like a bird. . .
She wings over earth. . .
She dances in fire. . .
For she is the Spirit, one with God in essence,
gifted by the Saviour in eternal love;
she is the key opening the scriptures,
enemy of apathy and heavenly dove.

midwife In some recent worship materials, God is the midwife who brings creation to birth. For the Iona community, the Third Person is the midwife who is perpetually birthing change.

From an evening liturgy of the Wild Goose Worship Group, 1999:

Comforter,
Disturber,
Interpreter,
Enthuser,
come, Holy Spirit.

Heavenly Friend,
Lamplighter,
Revealer of truth,
Midwife of change,
come, Holy Spirit.[37]

rain[38] In the early seventeenth century, Josua Stegmann composed a lengthy hymn invoking the Third Person, opening with yet a different figure of speech from nature: rain coming from the heavens to quicken our innermost hearts. ***Question:*** *Do current worshipers recognize this meaning of "quicken"?*

rock[39] In a stanza still sung in our time, Michael Schirmer's classic hymn "O Holy Spirit, Enter In" calls the Third Person "mighty Rock," a figure of speech for God found over twenty times in the psalms. In another biblical example of faith in the unity in the Trinity, some biblical texts call the First Person the rock, other places refer to the Second Person as the rock.

root In a recent translation of Hildegard of Bingen's "Antiphon for the Holy Spirit," the Spirit of God is called the "root of the world-tree."[40] This figure of speech recalls the pre-Christian religious image of Yggdrasil, the world tree that holds the universe together and is itself the root of all that lives.

rope[41] In the first century, Ignatius of Antioch, writing an epistle to the Ephesians, called Christ's cross a crane that hoists us up to God, with the Spirit being the rope that we use. ***Question:*** *What do you think about this inventiveness?*

soul of the church[42] Leonardo Boff cites a Brazilian hymn that calls the Spirit "the soul of the church." This figure emphasizes the absolute importance of the Third Person enlivening the community of the baptized.

sword[43] During the fourth century, Bishop Ambrose engaged in severe controversies within the church and between the church and society, and so we ought not to be surprised when he wrote of the Third Person as the sword of the word. "I came not to send peace, but the sword," Ambrose cites from Matthew 10:34.

tree of life[44] If Christians are granted the fruit of the Spirit (Gal 5:22), it is a small imaginative step that makes the Spirit the tree of life on which grows twelve kinds of fruit. So wrote Symeon the New Theologian in the tenth century of the Spirit who is planted in the hearts of believers, to flower into the virtues of holy living.

wild goose In Celtic tradition, the wild goose serves as a figure of speech for the Third Person. The wild goose is known to have surprising and unpredictable creativity; it attacks if threatened, is noisy, and is courageous. An ancient story tells of the geese warning the Celts of the approaching Roman troops, and thanks to the wild cackling of the geese, the community was saved. So it is that Christians are called to heed the cry of the wild goose.

> *From* A Holy Island Prayer Book:
>
> Great Spirit, Wild Goose of the Almighty,
> Be my eye in the dark places;
> Be my flight in the trapped places;
> Be my host in the wild places;
> Be my brood in the barren places;
> Be my formation in the lost places.[45]

wine Employing a sacramental image, Brian Wren calls the Third Person "wine of mercy at the feast."[46] Thus as we eat of the body of Christ, we drink of the life of the Spirit, and our very bodies feel the vibrancy of the vine of the divine. ***Question:*** *What is lost and what is gained, when wine is replaced with grape juice?*

Figures of Speech That Unite

Many of the figures of speech that we have here considered are traditional, the standard ways that Christians have imagined the Third Person. Wind, breath, dove, advocate, oil, dew, friend, helper: these figures of speech have been shared during worship for centuries. We might think about them as examples of the theological preference that the Spirit is experienced mainly in the assembled church, that the Third Person comes through the Second Person and is thus known and trusted especially when realized in the baptized community.

However, some of the figures we have seen are surprising, even idiosyncratic, and a few rather bizarre. Bernard of Clairvaux was insistent that the Third Person is the divine kiss. Symeon the New Theologian calls the Spirit "inaccessible sandal." John Bell praises the Spirit as the "enemy of apathy." Such unique figures suggest that the Third Person comes regularly, perhaps even primarily, to the individual, to the believer praying and praising in solitude, and that such a believer can feel called to share this personal imagery with the wider church. These figures of speech seem to fly directly from and to the mind of God, with little taming by the ecclesial community.

So it is that continually, over the decades and centuries, some believers have the task of making a weekly choice: what should we call the Third Person, given this Sunday's biblical readings, given this week's world news, given this gathered assembly? Each person who plans assembly worship must decide how classical and how innovative ought the language of the baptized to be. Furthermore, who in each assembly and in each denomination bears the responsibility of decision? As well, we must always recall that what is new to some members of a given community might not be new to the Christian church. It was Ephrem the Syrian, in the third century, who wrote about the church, "May the Holy Spirit desire to enter in its door to dwell and sanctify. For behold, She moves about to all the doors to see where She may dwell."[47] The doors through which the Third Person enters may not be the immense main portal of a famous cathedral to which tourists flock, but rather the maid's doorway going in and out of the hut of a believing recluse.

Allow me one further thought about the Spirit as she. Thinking about the tradition of binary language for humans, we might conclude that if the First Person is still referred to as *he*, then the Third Person can rightly be *she*. Or, given the fluidity of gender, we might relax into an alternation of pronouns, seeing both he and she as merely flawed and partial figures of speech for the divine. Or we might argue for multigendered language as the most profound linguistic way forward.[48] Or leaders of worship might concur with Flannery O'Connor, that people "think faith is a big electric blanket, when of course it is the cross," and thus might understand the language of worship as the means through which the baptized are called into a more profound faith, and so we might choose to invite worshipers into what might be disruptive texts.[49] However, concerning pronouns, there is a complication. (For liturgists, there is usually a complication.) For most contemporary worshipers, "he" still retains some of its historic usage as the pronoun of choice when gender is unknown, and so for some worshipers can be heard generically. "She" stands up and shouts, "Here I am," and she still wears essentialism. Perhaps it is long since time that those who call themselves *she* affirm their connection with the Trinity. But my continuing counsel is this: no pronouns for God, who is far beyond our differentiating categories. ***Question:*** *How many of you agree with me about this?*

We conclude this chapter by listening to Hildegard's twelfth-century "Sequence for the Holy Spirit."[50]

O fire of the Spirit, the Comforter,
Life of the life of all creation. . .
O breath of sanctity,
O fire of charity,

> O sweet savor in the breast
> and balm flooding hearts. . .
> O limpid fountain. . .
> O breastplate of life
> and hope of the integral body,
> O sword-belt of honor. . .
> O current of power permeating all . . .
> You are the song of praise,
> the delight of life. . . .

Hildegard prays with both classic biblical figures—fire and breath—and contemporaneous innovative imagery, sword-belt of honor. I take her work as a model of prayer.

6

THE THREE-IN-ONE, FIGURATIVELY SPEAKING

Triune identity, triune activity, triune imagery

CHAPTERS 3–5 HAVE described dozens of the countless figures of speech that Christians have used to designate the First, then the Second, and then the Third Person of the Trinity. In this chapter we will look at what might be called triple figures of speech, that is, ways that using three words in succession—the Trinity as A, B, and C—invoke and describe God.

When speaking to and of the Trinity, the Christian tradition has attempted the impossibility of articulating what is utterly incomprehensible. The triune God is a mystery, not as a puzzle that smart folks can solve but as a glimpse of unfathomable divinity, a statement of faith in an existence beyond our own. This is not a simple task. To propose appropriate language for this Wholly Other,

From Symeon the New Theologian, in the tenth century:

The Trinity is light and peace and joy,
life, food and drink, clothing, a robe,
 a tent and a divine dwelling,
the East, the resurrection, repost and
 a bath,
fire, water, river, source of life and a
 flowing stream,
bread and wine, the new delight
 of believers,
the banquet, the pleasure which we
 enjoy in a mystical way,
sun, indeed, without any setting, star
 always shining,
lamp that burns inside the dwelling
 of the soul.[1]

Christian theologians have developed especially two different methods of speech, traditionally referred to as identifying the immanent and the economic Trinity. To these two this chapter will add a third method, a technique marked by unity of imagery. ***Question:*** *Can we speak of "mystery" in our scientifically oriented culture?*

Many theologians have preferred use of only the phraseology that features the "immanent" Trinity, what this book is calling "triune identity." For these Christians, the most significant information conveyed by the naming of God is to make clear the relationship between Jesus and God.[2] Why do we worship Jesus as God? How does God embrace the mystery of the incarnation? According to this method, the triple figure of speech strives to articulate divine identity, who God is in God's very self, how the Three Persons relate to each other, how Jesus Christ fits into God. In this classic Christian speech, the Second Person of the Trinity, who is in some ways the center of the faith, stands between the First and the Third Person. This chapter will give examples of this method of Christological nomenclature continuing in our time.

However, through Christian history, a second method of addressing God has become important for believers. What has been termed the "economic" Trinity, what this book calls "triune activity," focuses on what God does for us.[3] What does the Trinity effect for humankind? Are there three different things, or one thing three different ways? Sometimes this method has been condemned by theologians as functionalism, as if the three-ness of God is denoted through three different and distinct functions, each Person of the Trinity with a unique task to fulfill, or as modalism, as if God takes on three different modes of operation throughout time. Yet it is not surprising that believers seek to honor God as the deity for them. They seek to understand how divine activity grants them salvation. This method of constructing figures of speech has become popular in recent decades, and our hymnals are filled with expressions of triune activity.

A note here, about the figure of speech "father." To those who care about triune identity, the primary message of "father" is that Jesus is remembered as referring to God as his father. Thus naming the First Person as "father" places the Second Person in the center of our access to God. Meanwhile, to those who care about triune activity, this figure of speech has become significant in prayer and praise, the "father" understood not as father of Jesus but of ourselves, God as the father of the baptized, or even the father of all humankind. Thus "father" is both God-as-God-is and God-for-us, a figure of speech for both triune identity and activity. In a similar way, the proposal by the twentieth-century theologian Karl Barth, referring to the Trinity as Speaker, Word, and Meaning, can achieve both triune identity and activity: Christ is the Word, spoken by the Father and interpreted by the Spirit, and it is as the Word that God is active for the salvation of the world.[4]

From Brian Wren, "How Wonderful the Three-in-One," in the twentieth century:

How wonderful the Living God:
Divine Beloved, Empow'ring Friend,
Eternal Lover, Three-in-One,
Our hope's beginning, way and end.[5]

There is yet a third method. We might think of the legend of St. Patrick, holding up a shamrock for believers, that they might see an image of the Three-in-One. A shamrock is not about either the identity or the activity of God. Rather, it is a metaphoric image of God, and this chapter will give other examples of images that are essentially single but also threefold, offered as figures of speech for the Trinity. In some cases, as with the shamrock, the incorporation of something "three" has become a metaphor for "one": the three-leafed shamrock becomes leaf.

Trinitarian Figures of Speech in the Scriptures

Matthew 28:19 The doctrine of the Trinity finds its origin in the Scriptures, and here we will survey only the several places that this happens linguistically. While various citations from Scripture can be seen as inferring the Trinity, we will begin with the straightforwardness of Matthew 28:19, "Go therefore and make disciples of all nations, baptizing them in the name of the Father and of the Son and of the Holy Spirit." Although the original source and date of this expression remains a point of scholarly debate, "Father, Son, and Holy Spirit" remains the primary naming of the identity of the Christian God.[6] Indeed, one theologian has claimed that those persons who do not concur that this naming is dogmatically mandated "belong to some other community."[7] In this naming of triune identity, Christ is the Second Person of the Trinity, centering the mystery of the divine. Although these three nouns have been canonized as the standard designation of divine identity, they remain linguistically figures of speech, which we discussed in chapters 3–5. God is something like a father, God is something like a son, God is something like a spirit. Who is God in God's self? Father, Son, and Holy Spirit, since the Son is the son of the Father, and the Spirit is the spirit of the Son. ***Question:*** *How has the language of "Father, Son, and Spirit" been explained to you?*

> *From Julia Foote, in 1886:*
>
> Had not the three-one God been with me,
> I surely must have gone beneath the waves.[8]

John 14:26 The fourth Gospel offers an alternate to this naming of divine identity. In John 14:26 Jesus is quoted as saying, "The Advocate, the Holy Spirit, whom the Father will send in my name, will teach you everything and remind you of all that I have said to you." It is almost as if this evangelist or a later editor is suggesting a figure of speech more concrete than "spirit," thus providing an anthropomorphic term with many known uses in the present culture. Yet the difficulty Christians have had in choosing the best translation of *paraklētos* has meant that some rendering of *pneuma* has become the dominant figure of speech for the Third Person.

Isaiah 9:6 The Bible also provides a passage that Christians might see as indicating the activity of the triune God. As believers assemble on Christmas Eve to celebrate the incarnation of God in Jesus Christ, the lectionary's first reading includes Isaiah 9:6, where we hear the miraculous child named "Wonderful Counselor, Mighty God, Everlasting Father, Prince of Peace." Although not laid out in the usual Trinitarian order, this list looks familiar to Christians: the mighty God is named everlasting father, prince of peace, and wonderful counselor. This description of God focuses on divine activity: God is to us like a father, but one who is everlasting, thus quite different from a regular father; God is like a prince of peace, son of a king who leads the people not to war, but to peace; and God is like a counselor who surprisingly stands by us with strong comfort. Christians can see in this passage in Isaiah one biblical example of a triple of divine activity.

2 Corinthians 13:13 In yet another passage, the Bible provides Trinitarian figures of speech that feature both divine identity and divine activity. The conclusion of 2 Corinthians is the Pauline benediction "the grace of the Lord Jesus Christ, the love of God, and the communion of the Holy Spirit be with all of you." We see here language of divine identity: the Lord Jesus Christ as the way into God and the gift of communion in the Holy Spirit. We encounter also the language of divine activity: who is God for us? Believers receive grace from the Second Person, love from the First, and communion with the Third. It is not surprising that this biblical citation has become beloved as a Christian blessing, indicating both the identity and activity of God granted to the faithful.

Identity Figures of Speech from Christians Past and Present

In each of these triples, the First and the Third Persons are in relationship with the Second, traditionally called the immanent Trinity.

Abba, Servant, Paraclete[9] In this proposal, included as an alternative blessing in *A New Zealand Prayer Book,* the triple figure of speech uses biblical language to state triune identity. The Second Person is the servant, an image taken from Isaiah and the Gospels; the First Person is named in relation to the Second, as the Abba of the servant; the Third Person is the one whom the Servant will send. We see also in other contemporary Trinitarian triples the substitution of Abba for Father. ***Question:*** *Does the nomenclature of this blessing rely on more biblical knowledge than worshipers have?*

the Father, the Son, the Holy Spirit, One God, Mother of us all[10] Well-known thanks to its use at the Riverside Church in New York City, this proposal reiterates the classic Trinitarian figures of speech yet adds a gloss of two additional phrases that address contemporary identity concerns: the misunderstanding that there are three gods is met by the words "one God," and the criticism that Matthean language is narrowly patriarchal is corrected by invoking the figure of Mother. A recent essay suggests that the words spoken during baptism be amended in a similar manner: while pouring the water, the presider's "Father" would be followed by a second voice, calling out an appropriate alternate figure of speech, such as "Mother, Giver of life," with the same pattern followed for Son and Spirit.[11] ***Question:*** *Would this practice diminish the sense of the classical divine name being a magical formula that effects baptism?*

Giver, Given, Gift/ing[12] Here the Second Person is the one given, with the First Person as the source of the gift and the Third Person as the ongoing Gifting.

kisser, kissed, the kiss[13] Bernard, abbot of Clairvaux, an eminent theologian and church leader during the twelfth century, taught that the Second Person was the one kissed by the First and that the Third Person is the kiss that is shared between the First and Second Persons. This figure of speech was central to Bernard's 86 sermons on Song of Songs, that biblical poem that does not mention God or the LORD even once. ***Question:*** *Has such a figure of speech any use in our time?*

> *From Ode 19, "The Cup of Milk," in the second-century* Odes of Solomon*:*
>
> The cup of milk was offered to me.
> And I drank it in the sweetness of the Lord's kindness.
> The Son is the cup.
> And the Father is He who was milked.
> And the Holy Spirit is She who milked Him. . . .
> The Holy Spirit opened Her bosom,
> And mixed the milk of the two breasts of the Father. . . .[14]

Lover, Beloved, Love[15] In the fifth century, Augustine coined what has become one of the most revered divine figures of speech, the First Person loving the Beloved, and the Third Person being the Love itself, now shared with believers. God is all about love.

Singer, Song, Breath[16] A hymn titled "The Singer and the Song" develops a creative figure of speech about triune identity: the center of all things is the Song Incarnate, which is now "our own song once more," with the Singer and the Breath praised as the source and the means of the Song.

Source, Truth, Inspiration A hymn titled "Praise the Spirit in creation" presents an abstract figure of speech that preferences the Second Person: the First Person is the Source of the Truth, and the Third is the Inspiration of the Truth, truth being what we most want and need.[17] Many other Trinitarian proposals replace Father with Source. ***Question:*** *Can abstractions such as "source" and "truth" work well as divine figures of speech?*

> *From Marguerite Porete, in* The Mirror of Simple Souls, *in the fourteenth century:*
>
> The Father is eternal substance; the Son is pleasing fruition; the Holy Spirit is loving conjunction. This loving conjunction is from eternal substance and from pleasing fruition through the divine love.[18]

Activity Figures of Speech from Christians Past and Present

In each of these proposals, the primary goal is for the Trinitarian language to connect in three ways with believers.

> *From Mechthild of Magdeburg, in the thirteenth century:*
>
> Lord, heavenly Father, you are my heart.
> Lord Jesus Christ, you are my body.
> Lord Holy Spirit, you are my breath.
> Lord, Holy Trinity, you are my only refuge and my eternal rest.[19]

Creator, Lover, Sustainer of the universe[20] In a twenty-first-century eucharistic prayer written for African Anglicans, "Creator" and "Sustainer of the universe" are especially appropriate designations, given that the prayer focuses praise on God's gift of the earth. The prayer then also names God as Lover of the individual believer.

Creator, Redeemer, Sustainer This triple figure of speech has received both considerable popularity and vociferous criticism, since it seems to suggest that each Person of the Trinity has one unique task to fulfill. Yet such a division of labor can be seen as theologically inappropriate: looking for example at Creator, each Person has been acclaimed in Scripture and the tradition as creator.[21] However, it may be that each of these three figures means to apply to all of the three. A further question is whether "sustainer" is a meaningful figure of speech.

hand, touch, cautery[22] In the sixteenth century, John of the Cross described God as a living flame of love and the transformation of the individual soul in union with the Trinity as a burning. For this experience of branding, the hand is the First Person, the touch is the Second Person, and the cautery—that is, the instrument responsible for the burning that leads to healing—is the Third. We must be careful around this God.

my judge, my witness, my advocate[23] In his poem "To Heaven," the seventeenth-century dramatist Ben Jonson appealed to God using judicial figures of speech, praying that despite his sins, God will once again be "my faith, my hope, my love."

The juridical imagery might remind us of a recurrent linguistic usage of St. Paul.

liberator, redeemer, emancipator[24] In the twentieth century, Walter Brueggemann saw throughout especially the Old Testament a God who attended to the needs of entire populations. These politically oriented figures of speech plead with God for "all those bondaged."

> *From Julian of Norwich, in her fifteenth-century A Revelation of Love:*
>
> I it am: the might and the goodness of the Fatherhood. I it am: the wisdom and the kindness of Motherhood. I it am: the light and the grace that is all blessed love. I it am, the Trinity. I it am, the Unity. I it am the high sovereign Goodness of all manner thing. I it am that maketh thee to love. I it am that maketh thee to long. I it am, the endless fulfilling of all true desires.[25]

maker, midwife, mother[26] One of the doxologies suggested for Christian use in the Uniting Church in Australia gives glory to "God, maker, midwife, mother." Alliteration is often a good idea to assist memory, and here three Ms present God as the one creating us, assisting at our birth, and raising us in love. Together, these three lean toward the female and bring us life.

memory, understanding, will[27] In the fifth century, Augustine proposed an anthropology that delineated memory, understanding, and will as the three primary functions of the human mind. And thus the very self of God, who created humans in the divine image, can be seen as memory, understanding, and will.

mother, brother, holy partner[28] In the final stanza of Ruth Duck's Trinitarian hymn "Womb of Life and Source of Being," characterized throughout by expansive figures of speech, God is both "Father, Spirit, Only Son," and our Mother, our Brother, and our holy Partner, "One-in-Three and Three-in-One" for us. Each of these three figures of speech expresses God's relationship to us as believers.

our mother, and daughter, and the holy of holies[29] In 1990, Bobby McFerrin concluded his "The 23rd Psalm" with this doxological expression. The holy of holies was a traditional translation of 2 Chron 3:10 for the most sacred inner section of the Jerusalem temple. ***Question:*** *Can Christians use this triple figure of speech in assembly worship?*

mother, lover, friend Sallie McFague's influential book *Models of God*[30] presents God as mother, lover, and friend. God births the believer, embraces the believer to live with God, and cultivates in believers the goal of being mother, lover, and friend to others and to the earth itself.

table, food, waiter[31] In her ecstatic prayer 12, recorded by her amanuensis on February 16, 1379, Catherine of Siena asks to come to know the eternal Trinity as the table that offers us the Lamb, who is the "most exquisite of foods for us," and the waiter who serves us this teaching. For Catherine, the Trinity comes to the faithful through the food of the eucharist.

our wealth, our treasure, our satisfaction[32] The "Blessing of Brother Leo" is ascribed to Francis of Assisi, who has become for many believers the model of Christian poverty. Here the Trinity is praised as being our wealth, the replacement of earthly treasure, and the presence of a satisfied life, an apt triple figure of speech from the poor man of Assisi.

wisdom, word, presence: A dismissal from a recent Australian worship resource blesses the departing assembly with God's Wisdom, God's Word, and God's Presence.[33]

> *From* Sundays and Seasons 2024,
> *Worship Texts for November:*
>
> The Ancient One, enthroned,
> the Crucified One, now risen,
> the Indwelling One, poured out,
> ✝ bless you now and forever.[34]

Unity Figures of Speech from Christians Past and Present

base tone, fourth, fifth[35] In 1927, Karl Barth used a musical figure of speech to describe God: the First Person is the base tone, that is, the tonic, in solfège "do," the Second Person is the fourth, "fa," and the Third Person the fifth, "sol." According to this figure of speech, the Persons collaborate with their distinct pitches to create a chord of perfect harmony.

dance[36] Written in 2002, Richard Leach's "Come, Join the Dance of the Trinity" is one of several recent hymns that celebrate divine *perichoresis,* the eighth-century theological imagery of the Persons of the Trinity interweaving with one another, as if dancing together, and inviting us to join in their everlasting dance.

embryo, chrysalis, butterfly, one divinity[37] In a prayer designed in the twentieth century for use at the Easter Vigil, Mary Kathleen Speegle Schmitt calls God "She Who Journeys with Us" and praises God with a triple figure of the butterfly. Some theologians might see this as an example of modalism. ***Question:*** *When is addressing a current concern more important than avoiding historic heresy?*

> *From Dante,* Paradise, *his vision of the Trinity, in the fourteenth century:*
>
> Within Its depthless clarity of substance
> I saw the Great Light shine into three circles
> in three clear colors bound in one same space;
> the first seemed to reflect the next like rainbow
> on rainbow, and the third was like a flame
> equally breathed forth by the other two.[38]

flame, brilliance, heat[39] In his discussion of "three names and one God," the fifth-century theologian with the startling name Quodvultdeus used a triple form of the image of fire as an example of the threeness of the divine name. "They work together," he wrote. "Thus when it is asserted that God made the world, the understanding is this, the Father in and through the Son and with the Holy Spirit."

fleur-de-lis[40] The thirteenth-century mystic Gertrude of Helfta used the figure of the fleur-de-lis to suggest the three in oneness of the Trinity—one stem, three leaves.

fugue[41] We might imagine that the interweaving of the Three Persons is a fugue, in which one musical motif is repeated in different voices, resulting in complex beauty.

greenness[42] Reading through the twelfth-century homilies that the Benedictine abbess Hildegard of Bingen delivered outside her convent as a self-appointed traveling preacher, we find that each Person of the Trinity is praised for *viriditas*, greenness. All creation contains the greenness of the Creator; Jesus heals the sick with his greenness; and the greenness of the Holy Spirit shows forth in our Christian life. So the triune activity is green, green, green, all for us.

marbled, white, red[43] In the twelfth century, Elisabeth of Schönau saw a vision of a triangular column sky high, one side white, one side red, and one side the color of marble. An angel told her that marble was the color of the divinity of the Father, white the color of Christ's humanity, and red the color of the Holy Spirit.

root, shoot, fruit[44] The third-century theologian Tertullian, who coined the phrase "three persons in one substance," proposed several analogies of the Trinity, this one able to be translated with an English rhyme. "Fruit" emphasizes the life of the believers granted by the Third Person.

rose bush, flower, fragrance[45] In his extensive defense of divine images, the eighth-century poet and theologian John of

Damascus describes his understanding how the brain receives and stores figures of speech. Among his several examples of Trinitarian images is God as a rose, its flower, and its fragrance. "Fragrance," an unseen dissemination of goodness, seems an apt figure for the Third Person.

sea of holiness, spring of salvation, cloud of mystery[46] In a thanksgiving prayer over the font, this twenty-first-century triple figure of speech expands on the life-giving activity of water. Another prayer in the same collection calls God ocean, river, and fountain. ***Question:*** *Is one of these better than the other?*

shamrock It was not until 1680 that a written account tells of Patrick in the fifth century evangelizing Ireland with the assistance of the three-in-one shamrock as a depiction of the Trinity. But perhaps a beloved legend need not search for documentation.

source, wellspring, living water[47] In his twentieth-century theological study of the Trinity, David Cunningham examines Trinitarian beliefs, virtues, and practices, and proposes this triple power of water as a many-faceted figure of speech for God.

Spirit-Sophia, Jesus-Sophia, Mother-Sophia[48] In her twentieth-century feminist masterwork *She Who Is*, Elizabeth Johnson CSJ presents the activity of Sophia—that is, Wisdom—as the primary and unifying figure of speech for the divine. In this formulation, we are led into the Trinity by means of the Third Person, Spirit, and so Spirit-Sophia comes first. ***Question:*** *Given the several persuasive proposals for the importance* *of the biblical language of Wisdom, why has it not become more commonly used in Christian worship?*

tree of life[49] In her prayer 17, recorded on March 3, 1379, Catherine of Siena spoke of the "High eternal Trinity" as the tree of life who made also us into trees of life, planted with "the fruit of loving," but which now must be grafted onto the Godhead for our life to be restored.

It should be noted that several of these unity figures might inspire artists and designers for appropriate triune imagery to be displayed in worship spaces or printed on liturgical materials. A fleur-de-lis, a shamrock, a tree of life, three shades of green: these may suggest the triune mystery in a simple yet profound way.

Identity, Activity, Unity: Why?

While there are indeed some Christians who give considerable attention to the Trinity, other Christians grant this theological pattern of believing little attention.[50] We might here consider what are some of the gifts that the church receives by means of its faith in the Trinity.

Those of us who treasure Trinitarian belief see in this doctrine an antidote to our culture's obsessive focus on the individual. Western society's dedication to self-determination, to autonomy of the individual, can well use the corrective of a Three-in-One god, a deity who is not a monad but rather is divine persons in mutual community. Indeed, to those who assert that "I am who I am," I say that I did not birth myself, grow my own food, nurture myself through childhood and into maturity, tend myself through illness. Being wholly and utterly alone signifies the end of my life, not the pattern for healthy living. As the French feminist philosopher Hélène Cixous wrote, "Impossible to think the one without the other and without either the one or the other," and she alters the usual inquiry "Who am I" by asking "Who are I?"[51] A triune God models for us the honest and realistic assertion that "I am who I are." Even our frustrating pursuit of self-knowledge can be comforted by the realization that the self is itself a complex of identities.

That there are worldwide calls for the abolition of the practice of solitary confinement demonstrates what we have learned: that humans are led into death by enforced solitary life. In Philadelphia in the nineteenth century, Quaker belief in the indwelling of God in each individual led to the practice of incarceration by solitary confinement, the idea being that the person isolated with God would find restoration. But this experience was halted because it led to insanity among prisoners. Christian doctrine proposes that not even God stands alone but intermingles within itself. One theologian who has focused her work on the Trinity writes, "it is communion, and not any notion that connotes autonomy, that informs and shapes our understanding of Christian spirituality."[52] Communion within God, communion with one another at the meal of communion: this is the central core of the Christian religion.

Focus on the Trinity encourages a Christological center to the faith. That the deity who saves is both a human who died and a divinity who animates everlastingly can assist us when facing death, for in the Trinity, death is part of life. We need not fear death but rather travel through it to God, upheld by the Third Person, accompanying the Second, honoring the First. Yes, it is true that an unreflective presentation of the Trinity can be at least stupefying and perhaps even harmful. But many of us pursuing a God who is worth our worship see in especially the last century of theological reflection a triune God as a fruitful tree under which to shelter, as an invincible castle to shield us from evil, as a welcome pathway for communal travel into meaning.

The Trinity on Sunday Morning

When considering ways that the Trinity can feature in assembly worship so as to meet to some degree our hopes for religion, it is best to begin by thinking about our own denominational and ethnic preferences. As the learned and clever book *The Unauthorized Guide to Choosing a Church* called each church's "Trinity Affinity," each assembly of worshipers has a historic or contemporary leaning toward the First, or the Second, or the Third Person of the Trinity, and it is helpful to rejoice at its strengths and to meditate on how to open wider our worship practices to the wholeness of the triune God.[53]

Those assemblies who use a three-year lectionary can welcome the first Sunday after Epiphany, dedicated to the narrative of the baptism of Jesus by John the Baptist in the Jordan River. What we discover is that the readings make of this Sunday at the beginning of January a celebration of the Trinity that, summing up the Christmas season, incorporates the community of faith into the triune God. In the Matthean Gospel in year A, Jesus hears the voice of God, receives the Spirit, and is acclaimed Son of God. Isaiah 42 proclaims that this divine one is a servant who brings justice to a new creation and light to the nations. As Luke writes in the Acts reading, we are promised forgiveness and so join in a life of divine service with Christ and one another in the Spirit.

In year B, the short account that narrates Jesus's baptism is likened to the creation story in Genesis 1, in which the Spirit of God hovers over the waters, the very waters in which we were baptized. And this baptism, says the reading from Acts, is not merely a washing away of sin. Rather, now bearing the name of Christ, we receive the Spirit, as did Jesus. Thus here at the outset of another calendar year, the Trinity is active in the lives of the faithful. In year C, once again, God is well pleased with Jesus, the First Person with the Second, and through the Third, with us as well. The poem from Isaiah walks us through the waters of baptism and the fires of life to welcome all the baptized as siblings in the faith. The responsorial psalm on this day for all three years is the startling Psalm 29. Thanks to this psalm, the voice of God heard at the Jordan is not a gentle message but a call from a king that thunders, breaking the cedars and flashing as lightning, the sound of overwhelming divine strength. ***Question:*** *Can the readings of these Sundays enliven the Trinity for your assembly?*

Each liturgical year also offers another celebration of the Trinity: the first Sunday after Pentecost is the culmination of the Easter season, the death and resurrection of Christ leading the faithful into the Trinity. In year A, the blessing that concludes the Matthean Gospel and the blessing with which Paul concludes 2 Corinthians are enhanced by the reading of Genesis 1: the very creation of the cosmos is set parallel to the creation of God's people through grace. The Trinity effects the creation of us all. The psalm is 8, which praises the majestic name of the God who set the moon and the stars in their courses and gave to the earth the wild beasts of the field. In year B, believers join Nicodemus in being born from the Spirit, "from above." Our worship joins with that of Isaiah, hearing the angels chant "Holy holy holy," and with that of Paul, calling God "Abba."

On this one Sunday, then, we are given two opposite expressions: the terror of Isaiah in the temple and the cry of the trusting child. The psalm is 29, in which the voice of God is stripping the forests bare. In year C, we hear Woman Wisdom rejoicing before God, Paul proclaiming our faith in the Trinity, and John testifying to Christ, who comes to us from the Father through the truth of the Spirit. It seems to me that preachers have multiple figures of speech with which to proclaim the Trinity on these Sundays, without recourse to feeble opening comments apologizing for some obstruse doctrine that they are assigned to consider.

Despite some of the creativity in divine naming that this chapter has discussed, I join those who assert that none of us has the authority to present a divine figure of speech that can wholly replace the classic "Father, Son, and Holy Spirit." Because of this, it might be that when the triune name is invoked in worship it may be pastorally wise that, inspired by the Riverside Church proposal, we cite both the classical name of God—Father, Son, and Holy Spirit—and a gloss of that name. By this method, we can hope to be simultaneously orthodox and creative. The gloss might be chosen to be especially appropriate to the church year, or to the specific occasion, such as a baptism, or to contemporary issues of ministry or mission. The Litany for Trinity Sunday, included in the 2017 Presbyterian *Book of Common Worship*, can be seen as offering suggestions for such a gloss.[54] Readers of this volume will recognize some of these figures of speech.

> Father, Son, and Holy Spirit: Glory to you forever!
> Speaker, Word, and Breath of Life: Glory to you forever!
> Font of Blessing, Living Water, Flowing River: Glory to you forever!

Compassionate Mother, Beloved Child, Life-Giving Womb: Glory to you forever!
Sun, Light, and Burning Ray: Glory to you forever!
Giver, Gift, and Giving: Glory to you forever!
Lover, Beloved, and Love itself: Glory to you forever!
Rock, Cornerstone, and Temple: Glory to you forever!
Consuming Fire, Dividing Sword, Overpowering Storm: Glory to you forever!
Rainbow of Promise, Ark of Salvation, Dove of Peace: Glory to you forever!
God who was, God who is, God who is to come: Glory to you forever!

Question: *How many of these glosses might you choose to enrich Trinitarian references in assembly worship?*

Here is another listing of Trinitarian figures of speech, some of the many offered by the Anglican priest Mary Kathleen Speegle Schmitt in her collection of prayers.[55] This list is far more unconventional than the one in the Presbyterian worship resource. ***Question:*** *How many of these would you choose as a gloss for Trinitarian speech in assembly worship?*

Heart's Desire, Passionate One, Bringer of Joy
Inhibiter of Darkness, Bringer of Light, Numinous One
Goddess in Terror, Goddess in Calm, Goddess All-in-All
Planter, Nurturer, Enlivener of All
Sorrowful Woman, Vulnerable One, Holy Comforter
Mother of All, Bread of Life, Cup that Overflows
Heavenly Scribe, Divine Word, Poet of Justice

A further option is for the assembly to sing together one of many recent Trinitarian doxologies characterized by inclusive or expansive language. Here for example are two such doxologies, written by Ruth Duck, and sung to the tune of Old Hundredth:

> Praise God the Father and the Son
> and Holy Spirit, always one,
> the God whose holy name we call,
> one God and Mother of us all.[56]

or

> Praise God, the Source of life and birth;
> praise God, the Word, who came to earth;
> praise God, the Spirit, holy flame;
> all glory, honor, to God's name.[57]

But no matter whether the classic Trinitarian figure of speech—Father, Son, and Holy Spirit—stands alone or is complemented by gloss or assembly song, we need always to heed the warning made by Julian of Norwich about any and all Trinitarian language. Discussing the meaning of the creedal phrase that the Son sits at the right hand of the Father, she added: "By this is not meant that the Son sitteth on the right hand beside his Father, as one man sitteth by another, in this life. For there is no such sitting, as I understand it, in the Trinity. But he sitteth on the Father's right hand: that is to say, right in the highest nobility of the Father's joy."[58]

Thank you, Julian, for "no such sitting," as our Trinitarian figures of speech for the First, Second, and Third Persons of the Trinity reign from thrones and sleep in the straw and take wing without restraint through the cosmos. For as the mystic Angela of Foligno wrote, "It is indeed the Trinity that has entered into you."[59] "You"—in English, at its root, a plural pronoun.

7

EXTENDED FIGURES OF SPEECH

More Than Single Words

Most of this volume deals with figures of speech that are single words. Chapter 1 delineates the genres in which these words are usually embedded: in similes, in metaphors, in epithets, in biblical parables and narratives. As if these were items on a ship's manifest, these figures of speech propose to be if not necessary, at least advisable cargo on our Christian journey. Chapters 2 through 6 list, categorize, and analyze such figures of speech, sometimes even in alphabetical order, one word at a time, creating a kind of thesaurus for Trinitarian faith. In some cases, two words are cited, the model and the qualifier—an example is "sweet Lord" as an English rendering of *Seňor*—since Christians may need to adjust a common noun with a surprising adjective to express more adequately their experience of the Trinity.[2] Chapter 6 deals with figures of speech that are linguistically triples, three interrelated terms that, as a tight unit, manifest the triune God.

> *From John Polkinghorne, twentieth-century theoretical physicist and theologian:*
>
> Since I am a Christian, the perspective that I adopt is Trinitarian.[1]

In order to deal more comprehensively with Trinitarian figures of speech, this chapter will now attend briefly to examples of such language that are amplified, what we might call extended figures of speech. Christians discover that it is not only individual words, by ones or twos or threes, that manifest the triune mystery: rather, the mystery is proclaimed by means of an entire unit of text. For such units of text we can use the traditional term "pericopes," biblical texts of perhaps ten or twenty verses that are proclaimed as a single unit during Christian worship. A pericope might be a complex poem from a prophet about the promises of God, or a Pauline proposal for recognizing the body of Christ, or a long narrative from the Gospels featuring Jesus. A pericope might be one of the parables of Jesus, interpreted as proclaiming a single surprising message, rather than containing a hidden allegory of meanings. In these pericopes, a reader's intense focus on some single word may well miss the theological point that the passage intended.

> *From* The Book of Margery Kempe, *in the fourteenth century:*
>
> She told him how sometimes the Father of Heaven conversed with her soul as plainly and as certainly as one friend speaks to another through bodily speech. Sometimes the Second Person in the Trinity, sometimes all Three Persons in Trinity and one substance in Godhead, spoke to her soul, and informed her in her faith and in his love.[3]

Especially in the Eastern churches, the pericope in Genesis 18 of the three visitors to Abraham and Sarah at Mamre has been interpreted as just such an extended figure of speech. As the tale progresses from "three men" to "my lord" to "you" (singular), to "yourselves" (plural), to "they," to "I" to "the LORD" and back to "the men," some Christians have recognized this passage not as a factual narrative but as a description of a mysterious encounter with the triune God, who is sometimes seen as three distinct figures, and sometimes heard as a single voice. In a beloved tradition of the Orthodox churches, icons of this story have shown these visitors as three angels, an angel being a messenger of the power and love of God. Recently some churches in the West have adopted this tradition, and one such icon may serve as the bulletin illustration on Trinity Sunday. (Shopping in Athens to purchase one such icon, I remarked to the shop keeper about the angels, and she exclaimed, indignantly, "Not angels—that's the Father, the Son, and the Spirit!" Indeed.) ***Question:*** *How has Genesis 18 been taught to you?*

Primary examples of such pericopes are the passion accounts of the arrest, trial, and crucifixion of Christ in the four Gospels. Since some of these events, for example the remarkable exchange between Jesus and Pilate, took place with no outside witnesses, it perhaps misuses the text if we omit focus on the whole passage as a single creedal figure of speech. For it is the passion narrative in its entirety that testifies to Jesus as the despised and rejected Messiah and to God as the one who brings life from death. Indeed, the doctrine of the atonement arises not by examining individual figures of speech embedded in the account, but rather by stepping back from the several chapters and engaging in a long-distance look at intertextual connections within the wider Scriptures. Theologians have investigated how the entire passion narrative might be what we are calling an extended figure of speech, encapsulating the relationship of the First to the Second in the Third Person of the Trinity and the connection of the Trinity to us. ***Question:*** *What would the evangelists of the synoptic Gospels say about the detail in John 18:6, when the arresting officers fall to the ground?*

In the magnificent chapter Hebrews 11, in which the Christian author cites the history of faithful Jewish believers and makes them models of Christian faith in Christ's cross and resurrection, we encounter a fascinating comment about Abraham. That in Genesis 22 Abraham was willing to offer his son Isaac to God is interpreted as if in obedience Abraham did indeed sacrifice Isaac. The author of Hebrews writes that "figuratively speaking, he [Abraham] did receive him [Isaac] back." That is, the reference to what was in fact not the sacrifice of Isaac is concluded for believers as if Isaac had been killed and been subsequently raised to life. The raising of Isaac, which was not factual, is "figuratively speaking" an example of what God effected for us through the resurrection of Jesus. For Christians, the ancient narrative of Abraham and Isaac finds its religious meaning by its "figuratively speaking" of the mercy of God. ***Question:*** *Is this narrative a wise choice for proclamation at the Easter Vigil?*

> *From Ephrem the Syrian, in the fourth century:*
>
> The scriptures are set up like a mirror;
> One whose eye is clear sees there the
> image of the truth.
> Set up there is the image of the Father;
> depicted there is the image of the Son,
> and of the Holy Spirit.[4]

One such extended figure of speech for the Trinity is the cosmogony in Genesis 1:1–2:4. Christians from early centuries asserted that the triune God did not originate at the incarnation. Rather, it was the triune God who created the cosmos, who was Trinity from before the beginning of time. It was taught that the Second Person of the Trinity was active in the words God spoke—"let there be light"—and the Third Person was active as the *ruah*, traditionally translated as "the Spirit of God," sweeping over the waters. Trinitarian belief has been muted when, in many current biblical translations, *ruah* is rendered as "the wind from God," "a mighty wind" that enters the narrative.

Question: *How much ought Christian biblical interpretation influence the Bible translation that is chosen for public worship?*

Contemporary Christians ought to inquire what benefit there is in the public proclamation of Genesis 1. At the least, the Genesis pericope is an extended figure of speech of the benevolent God, who is prior to the earth, outside of created things, who provided an ecology of life and death for all creatures, as well as companions, food and even rest for humankind. This depiction of God is presented, not line by line, but by means of the entirety of the cosmogony. It is because of its celebration of the miraculous beneficence of the God of life and death that Genesis 1 becomes the first biblical reading at the Easter Vigil, the resurrection being yet another creation.

The goodness of the cosmos for the sustenance of the human species that Genesis 1 describes can be recognized by Christians as mirroring the goodness of God; the words spoken by God can be received as the Second Person of the Trinity speaking light over and into all things; *ruah* can be best rendered so that Christians can hear there the movement of the Third Person over all things. What twenty-first-century Christians can receive in Genesis 1 is a mirror image of the Trinity, if they are willing to look for it there. Such a Trinitarian proclamation of Genesis 1 may help move it away from an unhelpful literalism into contemporary Christian faith.

Also other of the readings suggested for the Easter Vigil readings can be viewed as extended Trinitarian figures of speech. In the Revised Common Lectionary's suggested readings for the Easter Vigil is Isaiah 55, where we as Christians might encounter the First Person of the Trinity, inviting us to a feast on the mountain and calling us to life in the covenant. In the reading chosen from either Proverbs or Baruch, we Christians meet the Second Person, in Woman Wisdom teaching us truth, serving us bread and wine, and shining on us with her light. In Ezekiel 37, the Third Person is blowing life back into our dry bones, reassembling all the members into the risen body of Christ. The Trinity is with us, gathering us around the Easter fire.

> *From Gabrielle Bossis,* He and I, *in the twentieth century:*
>
> The Holy Trinity is in each one of you, more or less according to the space that you allow.[5]

Christian use of Song of Songs provides another example of seeing in a lengthy biblical passage a single extended figure of speech for the divine. Chapter 6 describes what to many Christians is the bizarre triune figure proposed by Bernard of Clairvaux in the twelfth century, that the Trinity is the one who kisses, the one kissed, and the kiss. We can credit Bernard for at least attempting to answer the question of what use this ancient erotic poem had for Christians. Bernard did as tradition had taught him, by looking not solely at the single verse of Song of Songs 1:2, but rather by reflecting on the entire Song of Songs as one extended figure of speech. The poem as a whole is seen as proclaiming the love of the triune God within the self of God, and consequently the love of the Trinity for us. If, on the other hand, the poem means to celebrate God's gift of sexual love, also in this case attention to the whole text is helpful. ***Question:*** *What would you suggest as a Christian use of the Song of Songs?*

The Trinity by Way of Myth

For decades, biblical scholars have analyzed the process by which Ancient Near Eastern myths and the legends of the residents of

Canaan and Mesopotamia were adopted by Israelites, adapted to speak of their own history, and incorporated into their sacred texts.[6] It appears, however, that church leaders or biblical scholars who are believers have worried that openly speaking of "myth" would cause the laity, many of whom equate myth with fantasy, to reject Christian doctrine as being untruthful. For whatever reasons, catechesis tends to rely on terms like "story" to label what a scholar calls "myth."

It may be in our time, however, that education renders the opposite to be the situation. For example, Egyptologists have demonstrated that the pyramids were constructed not by enslaved Israelites but, in centuries prior to biblical dating, by teams of the peasant population employed during the offseason, and such updates of Ancient Near Eastern history are readily available via various forms of media. In the present, the obvious inconsistencies between biblical accounts and factual evidence that is now discovered by scholarship and scientific inquiry may be more alienating to believers than would be pastoral instruction in this classic pattern of turning the world's myths and legends into devout testimony to God.

From Stephen P. Starke, a hymn at baptism, from the twentieth century:

In a wat'ry grave are buried
All our sins that Jesus carried:
Christ, the Ark of Life, has ferried
Us across death's raging flood.[7]

Popularly the word "myth" is indeed often used to designate an untrue story about the past, usually told by others than those who are presented, expressing an archaic worldview, and thus of only entertainment value in the present. Yet for over a century, biblical scholars have joined with historians, archaeologists, and psychologists to define myth in a positive way, as a traditional story describing the origin of the world, of natural or supernatural phenomena, or of human behavior, a story that may still be honored as expressive of the values of the community.[8]

Christians might find good use of biblical myths by reflecting on their possible Trinitarian meanings. For example, Genesis 2 is a comprehensive myth of the origins of human society. God has created a land with available water; a mature human formed out of soil; plenteous food; a pleasant place within the wider world; the animal kingdom, and human attention to it; a solution to human loneliness; and cooperative relationship between the monogamous man and the woman. But harsh realities of human life are evident: the neighbors have gold and onyx; death lurks; and there is something unsaid about nakedness. The myth concludes by stating that the man leaves home to live with the woman: clearly, the society originally responsible for this version of a myth of human origins was matrifocal. The myth both describes the goodness of God's creation and hints at the great needs that humans will encounter, for there is both praise for the earth as a garden and awareness that it will be harmed. (The myth continues in chapter 3 with more bad news.) For Christians, the myth can be seen as an extended figure of speech, if not of the Trinity, at least of God both as provider from the beginning and as monitor of human behavior in the future. Lutherans could recognize in this story both the law in human life and the gospel from the beginning and always at hand. ***Question:*** *Would you be glad for more use of the term "myth" in Christian catechesis?*

An example of a biblical myth that can function as an extended Trinitarian figure of speech are the flood accounts in Genesis 6:5–9:19. Scholars have compiled the many narratives of a primordial flood, found in ancient cultures the world over.[9] The fourth-century church historian Eusebius compared several different versions of the myth and judged that the biblical account was superior to the others, because of its relative antiquity.[10] Sadly, he was wrong about the dating of the Genesis versions. That the chapters in Genesis have combined two somewhat different accounts of Noah's flood is clear from the outset, when the repetitions are evident: in verse 6:5 the LORD saw the wickedness of humankind, and in verse 6:11, the earth was corrupt in God's sight. Most children's books recounting the myth omit a detail that is crucial to the meaning of some versions of the myth: that this destruction was divine punishment.

Although some Christians are intent on proving the historicity of the tale, in recent decades the flood story is repeatedly cited, as was common in the early church, as a figure of speech for baptism, in which God saves the people through water.[11] We see this practice of Ambrose in the fourth century, teaching the catechumens about baptism. Repeating to them the story of Noah and the flood, he concluded thus: "You see the water; you see the wood; you perceive the dove—and do you doubt the mystery?"[12] Of course the catechumens "see," not the water and the wood but rather the figures of speech. Several contemporary authors have borrowed this myth as an extended figure of speech for the Trinity, by addressing God as Rainbow, Ark, and Dove. As one option for a reading at the Easter Vigil, the flood story provides both a figure of speech for baptism and an exemplum of God bringing life from death. ***Question:*** *How ought prayers that praise God for the water of baptism cite the flood, even when it is understood not as Israelite history but as world myth?*

The Trinity by Way of Biblical Narrative

Not only the biblical redactions of world myth, but also biblical narratives, which are presented as if they are recordings of factual events replete with verbatim conversations, can at least be seen as extended Trinitarian figures of speech. An example is the narrative in John 20:19–31, which is proclaimed annually on the Sunday after Easter Day in the several versions of the three-year ecumenical lectionary. The disciples have gathered on the first day of the week, assembled by their faith in God; there they encounter the risen Christ, who breathes on them the Holy Spirit. Whether or not this narrative recalls factual history, it remains at least a Trinitarian figure of speech active in the community of the baptized. As believers continue over the centuries to gather on "the first day of the week," they together meet the risen Christ and share with one another the peace of the Spirit. The Christian liturgical gathering embodies the narrative by making the figure of speech into a communal action.

From Harry Emerson Fosdick, in New York City in the twentieth century:

Only the preacher proceeds still upon the idea that folk come to church desperately anxious to discover what happened to the Jebusites. The result is that folk less and less come to church at all.[13]

From Ephrem in the fourth century writing about the Diatessaron:

Many are the perspectives of God's word, just as many are the perspectives of those who study it. God has hidden in this word all kinds of treasures so that each one of us, wherever we meditate, may be enriched by it. God's utterance is a tree of life which offers you blessed fruit from every side.[14]

We can apply the same hermeneutic to the narrative of Luke 1:26–38. The story of the annunciation to Mary is far more beloved to many Christians than is the record of the disciples' gathering on the Sunday after Easter Day, and thus it may be that many believers are not interested in hearing about the legendary aspect of the Bible's nativity narratives. However, it may be that some believers would welcome the details presented, for example, half a century ago by the Christian biblical scholar Thomas Fawcett concerning the mythological character of the nativity stories.[15] In this pericope we encounter a version of a stereotypical religious and cultural legend, that an extraordinary leader experienced an extraordinary birth; that the mother conceived her child in some exceptional manner; that God sends angelic messengers to inform the faithful of their future; that the child is promised a throne; and that the woman acquiesces to her place in what the myth foretells. The biblical narrative presents to believers a way of seeing the belief that Jesus is acclaimed the Son of God.

Contemporary Christian believers of course have no recourse to some proof behind this narrative, but this story can be celebrated at least as an extended figure of speech. The Trinity is here, in greetings from God, who is named Lord; in the promise of the Son of the Most High; and in the power of the Holy Spirit. Christians can rejoice in this story especially in that the Trinity comes to bless the humble poor of the land, an unknown young girl, not distinctive in any way that society would recognize, and thus Mary herself is a figure of speech for the unworthy believer encountering divine mercy. ***Question:*** *Would appreciative reference to Mary as myth assist your celebration of Christmas?*

The Trinity by Way of Lectionary

When we speak of church tradition, we mean to denote the body of information, practice, and belief that is received by each generation and, having been judged worthy, is handed down to the next generation. Much that is said and done in Christianity is not valued tradition: it is inventive, localized, disconnected from the whole, short-lived. But textbook descriptions of religion would ideally feature especially those words and actions that reach the level of tradition, that have an honored past, respectful use in the present, and the promise of continuing meaning in the future. This volume has featured figures of speech from the great tradition, as well as others more transient, more limited. Some of these figures of speech would find place in an encyclopedia's essay on Christianity, and others not.

> *From Karl Rahner, in the twentieth century:*
>
> Shall I collect together all the words which praise your holy Name, shall I give you all the names of this world, you, the Unnamable? Shall I call you God of my life, meaning of my existence, hallowing of my acts, my journey's end, bitterness of my bitter hours, home of my loneliness, you my most treasured happiness?[16]

In much of the church, one of the primary conveyors of tradition is the lectionary, the list of biblical readings appointed for public worship. Some of the worldwide denominations expect or at least urge their congregations to use only their approved lectionary, since the idea is that the tradition of the faith is best contained within and nurtured by a distinct set of biblical passages. It is presumed that these choices were made by the collaboration of devout believers with considerable knowledge of church history, contemporary theological developments, and revered popular pieties. Even for those church communities that grant to the current minister full authority to select the biblical readings for assembly gathering, the assumption is that essential church tradition is conveyed through the chosen biblical passages, and that these passages are filled with the Spirit of God to inspire and uphold the faith of the community.

We can define lectionary as the canon within the canon, the selections of pericopes essential for the planting and the growth of the spirituality of the baptized. Lectionaries are authoritative storehouses of Christian tradition, which is why a change in one's lectionary is a momentous church event. The ecumenical three-year lectionaries have now had over fifty years of regular use, and we are growing into the tradition of the many Christian figures of speech that they present. ***Question:*** *How many of figures of speech listed in the index of this book are included in your church's lectionary?*

One obvious aspect of the three-year lectionaries is that they contain nearly three times more biblical passages than did one-year lectionaries. In comparison with historic church tradition, these lectionaries include more Israelite legends, more poems from the Old Testament, more instruction from the epistles, more stories about Jesus, more variation in narrative details, with even disagreements within scriptural accounts allowed to surface. Thus these lectionaries provide a substantially larger thesaurus for the faith than was previously maintained, a much longer manifest to indicate the cargo brought aboard the ship of the church. We can contrast a lectionary that featured one partial yet preferred passion narrative with the three-year lectionary, in which over three years all four passion accounts are proclaimed in full. It will take many cycles of this process to reach its goal of instilling more figures of speech that can enrich the church's

Christology. ***Question:*** *What is one pericope that you think ought to be in the lectionary that for some reason has been omitted?*

Religions present various methods of maintaining tradition, of sacralizing the vocabulary of faith. One technique available for controlling religious vocabulary is to authorize the sole use of a dead language, the immobility of its words ensuring that nothing new can threaten. Much of Christianity, instead, established scriptural lectionaries, judged as exemplary compendiums of sacralizing speech and recommended reading lists for the faithful, and it authorized translations of the Bible's countless figures of speech, figures that fill the linguistic gap existing when humans attempt to speak of the divine. Into the linguistic lacuna come words and phrases that do the best they can. Linguists use the term *catachresis* to label a word that, while admittedly inappropriate, meets a need created by the lack of an appropriate word. Catachresis fills a hole in the sentence, the inadequate borrowed term being necessitated because of the lack of an available appropriate word. "LORD/Lord" is one such catachresis. "Father" is another. If we cannot describe precisely how good is God's grace, we can choose a metaphor, even if mixed, to praise "honey from the rock" (Ps 81:16), piling up words into the linguistic lacuna.

> *From Symeon the New Theologian, hymn 6, in the tenth century:*
>
> How are you at once the source
> of fire,
> how also the fountain of dew?[17]

The remarkable anonymous fourteenth-century classic text titled *The Cloud of Unknowing* asserts that humans have no direct access to the divine. It is as if between the seeker and God there is a cloud of unknowing, a darkness that obscures our vision. Writing about how to pierce that darkness, how to get through the cloud to reach God, the author advises the practice of contemplation. Yet although referring to the Ark of the Covenant as "a figure of contemplation," that unknown author warns that even our faculty of imagination has been harmed by sin, and so it cannot be relied upon to lead us to God.[18] Adding to that author's list of the sins that distance humans from God is the very reality of language: words themselves and the spaces between them are part of the cloud that obscures.

In Revelation (8:1) is the startling sentence, "There was silence in heaven for about half an hour." So let us grant the author of *The Cloud of Unknowing* half an hour of silence. But even the medieval mystics in their discipline of silent contemplation were assembled several times each day for communal prayer using the figures of speech in the Psalter. This volume has urged not the silence of individual contemplation but rather the words and phrases of Scripture and of the texts and hymns used in worship as ways to receive the mercy of God, despite whatever cloud exists. Indeed, it may be that the Third Person of the Trinity is there, as dew, as cloud, ready to re-immerse us with the waters of baptism and bring us together into the presence of God.

Figures of speech are a linguistic form that can excel in making and strengthening communal bonds. Imagine a Sunday assembly: preschoolers coloring the bulletin, the partially deaf aged, women, men, and the nonbinary, every skin color, several ethnic origins, varying degrees of expertise in the vernacular, newly baptized Christians, church members who have not missed a Sunday in many years, persons in joy, persons in great grief, one worshiper grateful to be present, another much preferring to be at home doing the laundry. ***Question:*** *How in the world can words speak divine mystery to these many persons at once?*

The lectionary tries. Take, for example, the readings in the Revised Common Lectionary for proper 6 in year B. In the Ezekiel reading, God is the lord who is also a gardener, planting a tree. God is, surprisingly, not some god of nature but rather is reversing the natural order of things, making the high low and the low high. And so, Christians will think of the cross, the low tree made high. In the psalm response, God is named the Canaanite "Most High" and "rock." The assembly is invited not just to sit there but to "shout for joy." The people are likened to the great cedars of Lebanon, trees now transplanted into the temple, bearing fruit long after they could personally do so. In the reading from 1 Corinthians, we affirm that we walk not by sight but by faith, in both Christ the judge and Christ the lover. In the triune God—this is Christians who are listening—everything, even the stuff of religion, has become new. In the reading from Mark, God is likened to—or is—a kingdom in which seeds grow into a harvest—we are soon to be offered some bread and wine. And God is like, or is, the mustard seed from which comes a planting with such grand branches that it can welcome the birds of the air. As well, we will sing several hymns that develop this figure of speech. So it is that in the lectionary, each Sunday has its own parade of figures of speech, interweaving with one another, offering its distinctive vision of the God we worship and of the community that is gathered.[19]

Welcoming or Resisting Change

While church tradition may pride itself especially on those words that have been spoken for two thousand years, the living church understands that all our words have a future in a world that is changing all the time. Periodically the church has experienced great change, while in other time periods very little. One gladsome aspect of biblical figures of speech is their ability to open up a text to continuing revelation. Each century, each tradition, each reform has seen newness in God by exploring figures of speech. Doctrine has developed and devotion has deepened as Christians have prayed and probed biblical figures of speech. The practice of weekly preaching demonstrates the conviction that understanding Scripture and tradition is an ongoing process, and what one preacher saw last year can be amplified or altered the following year. That figures of speech often juxtapose at least two different things at once, layering the new onto the old, is a mark of the power of metaphor to advance human communication.[20] Old categories are broken apart, and the community sees something in a new way.

An example of this process concerns the biblical term *adelphoi.* Granting the patriarchal linguistic patterns of the cultures in which Christianity arose, it seems to have been quite appropriate to address a mixed audience as "brothers." At the outset of Christianity, the use of this familial category was a startling figure of speech to denote the new status of each person in the community of the baptized: members were now in a new family, formed by the Spirit in the resurrection. In the mid-twentieth century, many churches translated this term as "brothers and sisters," since it is evident that women were participants in those assemblies and that, in our time, manners called for addressing both. Yet one cultural habit of listing women first, as in "Ladies and gentlemen," was not selected as a translation of biblical speech. Moving on into the twenty-first century, some churches hope to limit, if not end completely, the habit of binary categories for humankind. Thus, hymnal committees must now ponder the many texts that refer to "men and women," and lectionaries suggest rendering the biblical "brothers" as "my dear family." The Second Person is not only "a brother" but also the genesis of the dear family of God.

One anthropologist describes the language of ritual as being "not entirely encoded by the performers."[21] That is, ritual actions and texts are somehow beyond ready and facile understanding, their meaning and significance continuously unfolding. What is continuously unfolding for Christians is a compendium of figures of speech. Normally, figures of speech are layered in such a way that a variety of participants each see what they are able to see, to hear what they can decipher. As the motley group receives the multivalent figures of speech, they are brought into one assembly, and by means of communal ritual responses, can speak the same words together. Those who regularly assemble share common memories: they remember the last time that biblical passage was proclaimed, they recall the hymns sung at baptism last Easter. Their memories assist in uniting them, over the years, over the weeks. That figures of speech are not entirely encoded by those present makes the unity of the assembly more possible, with an endless list of human individuals being held together in the figure of speech "the body of Christ." While being held into one, each worshiper's consciousness is free to go where the figure leads, and for each worshiper, the destination may be unique. Yet it is not so much "I," but, gladly, the "body of Christ" in which I am participant that has assembled for praise and prayer. ***Question:*** *How is the body of Christ present over Zoom?*

Nonetheless, an instructive linguistic study titled *Figuratively Speaking* (!) indicates that the benefit of figures of speech assumes the mutual recognition of the intention of the texts.[22] Since figures of speech have resonance that can be wide and deep, the users are bonded to one another by means of a communal sharing of the meaning of the situation and its vocabulary. The more biblical, traditional, and innovative figures of speech that a Christian community refers to and relies upon, the more catechesis and continuing formation are required.[23] To assume that a newcomer would know what even "the Son of God" means is to minimize the complexity in interpreting how religious figures of speech actually function.

The rising popularity of the practice of the adult catechumenate demonstrates the current recognition of the need to provide for seekers at least some assistance in participating in the figures of speech common to Christian worship. The assembled participants are called to recognize and appreciate the context in which the figures of speech are utilized. Were an uninformed visitor to assume that, for example, the context is entertainment, the purpose of figures of speech could be wholly misconstrued. On the other hand, if the group that is sharing these figures of speech intends fundamental and existential response, if Sunday worship is about "reaching the depths," somehow that intention must be made clear to all, especially in a society that prefers the personally casual.[24] Historically it was the preaching that was assigned this task. It remains to be seen whether preaching that focuses on personal reflections of the speaker can deliver adequate biblical signposts for the whole assembly. Perhaps the increasing practice of calling the children forward for an age-appropriate message could each week feature the figure of speech embedded in that day's scripture readings. ***Question:*** *Given all this, how ought Christians to evangelize?*

From Rachel Mann, "Credo," in the twenty-first century:

. . . If God, if if if, if God
Is to be claimed as lover
I must multiply names:
Pneuma, The Three-in-One,
Mother, Tetragrammaton,
Al-Wajid, Bhagavan, Diabolos,
Jesus, Jesus puts a tongue
Into my mouth, I Am.[25]

However, figures of speech can also divide, perhaps for good reason. Language inappropriate for assembly worship may be introduced. Prayers may be used not to unite the assembly in address to God but to force a desired change in spirituality. Visitors can be bewildered by what they judge to be only a specialized opaque vocabulary. Ecumenical interaction may encounter speed bumps along the way. Members of the community can advocate Sunday use of only their personal favorites or of the figures of speech memorized in their childhood as wholly adequate for their adult selves. Local clergy can, in one direction or another, disagree with the linguistic patterns adopted by their wider church. Parish members can—and will—debate the balance between traditional and innovative figures of speech. Indeed, many assemblies of believers have their own memories of communal controversy when an updated liturgical order was introduced or new hymns appointed, and returning worshipers were displeased with unfamiliar figures of speech. To the extent that contemporary Westerners prefer facts to figures of speech, the unique religious power of even biblical language will be minimized. It is intriguing that the fourth evangelist, after introducing and elaborating on several dozen figures of speech for the Second Person, bemoans in chapter 10 the community's inability to interpret it: "Jesus used this figure of speech with them, but they did not understand what he was saying to them." We smile at this aside of the evangelist, who is however speaking about us.

> *From Emily Dickinson, #18, in the nineteenth century:*
>
> In the name of the Bee —
> And of the Butterfly –
> And of the Breeze—Amen![26]

***Question:** Is Dickinson's poem a Trinitarian invocation?*

A word about that prayer treasured by Christians—recorded in two different versions in the Gospels, repeatedly over the centuries translated into countless languages, with newer versions resisted by many pious believers, called by some Christians "the Lord's Prayer" and others "the Our Father," and honored in the religion as the preeminent prayer of the baptized, this prayer includes several figures of speech for the divine.[27] God is "our." God is "father." God is "in heaven," whatever that might mean to us. God is identified with a sacred name, but what is that name? God has a kingdom: is God a king? Then come verbs: God gives bread, forgives sins, saves us, and delivers us. In the addendum, we attribute to God kingdom and power and glory. What does all this mean? Meanwhile, many Christians, having been taught that these words were given to the church by Jesus himself, honor this prayer as being especially sacred, too holy to touch. It is hoped that a Christian community, having undertaken its necessary homework of biblical study and sufficient theological reflection, can come to consensus concerning a contemporary rendering of these complex figures of speech, as our liturgy tries its best to speak the mystery of God.

A Manifest That Manifests

The hope of the Christian community, from the crucifixion and resurrection of Jesus to our gatherings next Sunday, is that figures of speech can indeed manifest the mystery. Not entirely, of course: that is one hope for what the creed calls "life everlasting"—itself an oxymoron, since "life" lives and dies, rather than continuing eternally. But in the liturgy we can see God's backside; we can touch the fringe of Jesus's cloak; we can breathe in a holy yet violent wind. To some degree, we can share with other Christians, not just teachings about but instead "the experience of God the Father, the experience of Christ, and the experience of the indwelling Holy Spirit."[28]And for that experience we are in the first place served by exposure to the biblical plethora of figures of speech, some proclaiming divine majesty, some announcing God's servanthood, some describing an amorphous surprise. That triune experience is upheld by music, art, vesture, gesture, movement, projections, catechesis. But in Christianity, that experience is grounded in the word and in the words about that word.

In 1968 the author and visual artist Seymour Leichman published a remarkable children's book titled *The Boy Who Could Sing Pictures*. Ben had a mysterious talent, that when he sang, the words came alive, and the people could actually see before them what his words said. In his land, the poor people suffered greatly from poverty and hunger and the cruelty of the King, but when they heard Ben sing, they found comfort and joy in the miracle of his song, for suddenly they could see the farmer's harvest, and the doves, and the rainbow. At the end, Ben "sang colors they had never seen, in a land they had never seen. . . . He sang sugar cane from another country, melons and cherries and all summer fruit in the winter snow, still fresh and good. . . . And oxen and warm fire and the sea gulls along the shore. And on and on he sang the Promised Land. The weary, he sang rested. The hungry, he sang full. The cold, he sang warm. And the great sadness, he sang all away."[29]

You might be able to find a copy of this book and enjoy the entire story. But perhaps even this short excerpt suggests how Christians experience the divine figures of speech. The language that Christians use in addressing and describing God are just such figures that are sung by the Bible, the liturgy, the hymns and meditations and the prayers of the baptized. In the mercy of the First Person, in the life of Second Person, and in the power of the Third Person of God, those figures give rest and food and warmth to the world. We do well to honor those figures, to translate them into our tongue, to concur on more of them, and to share them with the suffering world as best we can.

We are back to the burning bush. The "flame of fire out of a bush" needs to be described, as best can be, by words. The figure of a bush, blazing but not consumed, is, for Trinitarian Christians, the inscrutable majesty of fire, the word that names the divinity, and a burning compassion for all who suffer. We gather as close as we can to the fire. Its sparks are flying into the air, beyond our grasp, but we are transfigured by its heat. Honoring the burning bush, we might enjoy singing one of the recently composed Trinitarian hymns. There is Ruth Duck's "Womb of Life and Source of Being,"[30] which cites many figures of speech, including both the classic "Father, Spirit, Only Son" and the innovative "Mother, Brother, holy Partner." There is Thomas Troeger's "Source and Sovereign, Rock and Cloud,"[31] which lists forty biblical figures of speech for God—forty being the time throughout the Bible during which we await God.[32] But as we wait, we choose one figure of speech after another for our praise and our petition.

> *From Thomas Merton, in* Seasons of Celebration, *in the twentieth century:*
>
> Christianity is not so much a body of doctrine as the revelation of a mystery.[33]

It is disconcerting to conclude this study of Trinitarian figures of speech, for I know that once this book goes to press, I will encounter some images and expressions that I ought to have included. I could have given more focus to the works of theologians. I may have missed your favorites. But instead of more and more Trinitarian figures of speech, here I can only repeat the final remark of the fourth evangelist, "that the world itself could not contain the books that would be written." So, for now, this is enough.

AFTERWORD

AS PART OF Sunday worship, many churches include a comprehensive set of intercessions that pray for all in any need. Usually in the Western church these prayers are addressed to the First Person of the Trinity through the Second in the Third, but here is a set that is addressed to the Three-in-One and features objective figures of speech for the triune God. Each petition is succinct yet is best served by a moment of silence before and after. You are free to reproduce this prayer, to amend it in any way, or to let it inspire your own intercessions.[1]

Let us pray to God, Father, Son, and Spirit—our Source, our Sustenance, our Song—for all in any need.

> O God, for the church we pray:
> God our Water, renew the baptized each day with your grace.
> God our Bread, nourish us to be your one body in the world.
> God our Fire, inspire us for fervent devotion and faithful service.
>
> For the earth we pray:
> God our Sun, sustain with your might the life of our universe.
> God our Rainbow, restore beauty and vigor to what has been damaged.
> God our Garden, maintain fruitful places for us and for all animals to inhabit.

For the nations we pray:
God our Shield, protect us from conflicts, without and within.
God our Cornerstone, preserve the democracies of the world.
God our Mansion, establish justice for each person in our land.

For all in need we pray:
God our Storehouse, provide for those who are poor or hungry.
God our Tree of life, grant healing to those who are sick or suffering.
God our Key, free those who are oppressed or enslaved.
God our Ship, accompany all migrants and travelers.
God our Lamp, guide those who are lost in any way.
God our Fortress, keep safe those whose names we call out to you here: . . .

O God—our Dawn, our Day, our Darkness—in you is our beginning, our lifespan, our ending.

Receive our thanksgivings,
accept our petitions,
and manifest your mystery to us all, now and forever.
Amen.

NOTES

Foreword

1. Gail Ramshaw Schmidt, "Lutheran Liturgical Prayer and God as Mother," *Worship* 52 (1978): 517–542.
2. For example, see Gail Ramshaw, *Letters for God's Name* (Minneapolis: Seabury Press, 1984), reissued as *A Metaphorical God: An Abecedary of Images for God* (Chicago: Liturgy Training Publications, 1995); *God beyond Gender: Feminist Christian God-Language* (Minneapolis: Fortress Press, 1995); *Pray, Praise, and Give Thanks: A Collection of Litanies, Laments, and Thanksgivings at Font and Table* (Minneapolis: Augsburg Fortress, 2017); and *Blessing and Beseeching: Seventy Prayers Inspired by the Scriptures* (Minneapolis: Fortress Press, 2022).
3. John Donne, "XIX. Expostulation," *Devotions upon Emergent Occasions* (n.p.: Jefferson Publication, 2015), 76.

Chapter 1

1. *A Short Explanation of Dr. Martin Luther's Small Catechism: A Handbook of Christian Doctrine* (St. Louis, MO: Concordia Publishing House, 1943), 47–48.
2. John Updike, *Collected Poems 1953–1993* (New York: Knopf, 1993), 20–21.
3. See Daniel B. Stevick, *Beyond Fundamentalism* (Richmond, VA: John Knox Press, 1964) for a discussion of the problems of literalism in Christian speech.
4. Ambrose, *The Sunday Sermons of the Great Fathers*, vol. 1, trans. and ed. M. F. Toal (Chicago: Henry Regnery, 1955), 213.

5. See for example Henry M. Morris and Martin E. Clark, *The Bible Has the Answer,* rev. and exp. ed. (Green Forest, AR: Master Books, 1987), 295.
6. Janet Soskice's *Naming God: Addressing the Divine in Philosophy, Theology and Scripture* (Cambridge, UK: Cambridge University Press, 2023) deals with God and Christ, but not the Trinity.
7. Gertrude of Helfta, *The Herald of Divine Love* (New York: Paulist, 1993), 55.
8. Ian T. Ramsey, *Religious Language: An Empirical Placing of Theological Phrases* (London: SCM Press, 1957), 49–61.
9. Justin Martyr, "The First Apology," in *The Ante-Nicene Fathers*, ed. Alexander Roberts and James Donaldson (Grand Rapids, MI: Eerdmans, 1979), 1:185.
10. See Robert W. Jenson, *The Triune Identity: God according to the Gospel* (Philadelphia: Fortress Press, 1982), 12–13, for the claim that "Father, Son, and Holy Spirit" is the proper name of God. Note also the fetching title of an essay by Alvin F. Kimel Jr., "A God Who Likes His Name: Holy Trinity, Feminism, and the Language of Faith," in *Speaking the Christian God: The Holy Trinity and the Challenge of Feminism,* ed. Alvin F. Kimel Jr., (Grand Rapids, MI: William B. Eerdmans, 1992), 188–208.
11. See R. Kendall Soulen in *Divine Names(s) and the Holy Trinity: Distinguishing the Voices*, vol. 1 (Louisville: Westminster John Knox Press, 2011) for a sustained discussion of the tetragrammaton as the primary Christian name of God.
12. Rabbi Arthur Waskow, "Excerpt from 'Why YAH/YHWH,'" www.haggadot.com/clip/excerpt-why-yahyhwh-rabbi-arthur-waskow (accessed February 1, 2024).
13. See James E. Griffiss, *Naming the Mystery: How Our Words Shape Prayer and Belief* (Cambridge, MA: Cowley Publications, 1990) for consideration of issues involved in speaking mystery.
14. John of Damascus, *Three Treatises on the Divine Images*, trans. Andrew Louth (Crestwood, NY: St. Vladimir's Seminary Press, 2003), 26.

15. Brian Wren, "When God Is a Child," *Bring Many Names* (Carol Stream, IL: Hope Publishing Company, 1989), #34.
16. Ramshaw, *Blessing and Beseeching,* 32.
17. See G. B. Caird, *The Language and Imagery of the Bible,* rev. ed. (Grand Rapids, MI: William B. Eerdmans, 1980), 144–159, for more discussion of the differences between simile and metaphor.
18. Denise Levertov, "Flickering Mind," in *Upholding Mystery: An Anthology of Contemporary Christian Poetry*, ed. David Impastato (New York: Oxford University Press, 1997), 122–123.
19. Paul Ricoeur, *The Rule of Metaphor: Multi-disciplinary Studies of the Creation of Meaning in Language*, trans. Robert Czerny (Toronto: University of Toronto Press, 1977), 24.
20. See for example Sallie McFague, *Metaphorical Theology: Models of God in Religious Language* (Philadelphia: Fortress Press, 1982).
21. Charles Halton, *A Human-Shaped God: Theology of an Embodied God* (Louisville, KY: Westminster John Knox Press, 2021) argues that God is both transcendent and a being "very similar to humanity," with a human-like body and emotions, and that such speech is not metaphor but accurate description.
22. Daniel B. Stevick, "The Language of Prayer," *Response* 3 (1976): 9.
23. See Raymond E. Brown, *The Gospel According to John (i–xii),* The Anchor Bible (Garden City, NY: Doubleday & Company, 1966), vi–lvii.
24. Caird, *Language and Imagery of the Bible*, 184–185.
25. Charles Causley, "I am the Great Sun," in *Collected Poems 1951–2000*, rev. ed. (London: Picador, 2000), 57.
26. See Thomas Fawcett, *The Symbolic Language of Religion* (Minneapolis: Augsburg Publishing House, 1971), 177–181, for sympathetic consideration of angels.
27. Griffiss, *Naming the Mystery*, 127.
28. Gregory of Nazianzus, "The Fifth Theological Oration: On the Spirit," in *A Select Library of Nicene and Post-Nicene Fathers*, 2nd series, ed. Philip Schaff (Grand Rapids, MI: Eerdmans, 1956), 7:320.

29. See for example Rosemary Radford Ruether, *Sexism and God-Talk: Toward a Feminist Theology* (Boston: Beacon Press, 1983); Elizabeth A. Johnson, *She Who Is: The Mystery of God in Feminist Theological Discourse* (New York: Crossroad, 1992); Gail Ramshaw, *God beyond Gender: Feminist Christian God-Language*; and Ruth C. Duck and Patricia Wilson-Kastner, *Praising God: The Trinity in Christian Worship* (Louisville, KY: Westminster John Knox Press, 1999). Much of this material needs to be reconsidered in light of the recent more fluid understanding of gender.
30. See Elizabeth Rankin Geitz, *Gender and the Nicene Creed* (Harrisburg, PA: Morehouse Publishing, 1995).
31. Jacque B. Jones, "We Long to Know Her," *Voices Together* (Harrisonburg, VA: MennoMedia, 2020), # 44.
32. Emily Dickinson, "1258," in *The Complete Poems of Emily Dickinson*, ed. Thomas H. Johnson (Boston: Little, Brown, and Company, 1960), 550–551.
33. For an account of Karl Rahner's objections to the label "person" and a defense of that term, see Robert Letham, *The Holy Trinity: In Scripture History, Theology, and Worship* (Phillipsburg, NJ: P&R Publishing Company, 2004), 294–295 and 458–464. For a wider discussion of "person," see Vincent Brümmer, *Atonement, Christology and the Trinity: Making Sense of Christian Doctrine* (Burlington, VT: Ashgate Publishing Company, 2005), 97–112.
34. See for example the exemplary work of Thomas Fawcett, *Hebrew Myth and Christian Gospel* (London: SCM Press, 1973).
35. See for example Sallie McFague TeSelle, *Speaking in Parables: A Study in Metaphor and Theology* (Philadelphia: Fortress Press, 1975).
36. Irenaeus, "Against Heresies," *Early Christian Fathers*, trans. and ed. Cyril C. Richardson (New York: Macmillan, 1970), 382.
37. For a study of these lectionaries, see Gail Ramshaw, *Word of God, Word of Life: Understanding the Three-Year Lectionaries* (Minneapolis: Augsburg Fortress, 2019).
38. See William P. Brown, *Seeing the Psalms: A Theology of Metaphor* (Louisville: Westminster John Knox Press, 2002) for an

elucidation of some of the primary metaphors that come into Christian speech from the psalms.

39. See James K. A. Smith, *Who's Afraid of Postmodernism? Taking Derrida, Lyotard, and Foucault to Church* (Grand Rapids, MI: Baker Academic, 2006).
40. Les Murray, "Poetry and Religion," in *Upholding Mystery*, 127.
41. For a lucid description of the blended theory of cognitive linguistics, see Stephen R. Shaver, *Metaphors of Eucharistic Presence: Language, Cognition, and the Body and Blood of Christ* (New York: Oxford University Press, 2022), 1–105.
42. See George Lakoff and Mark Johnson, *Metaphors We Live By* (Chicago: The University of Chicago, 1980).
43. See for example Robert Masson, *Without Metaphor, No Saving God: Theology after Cognitive Linguistics* (Walpole, MA: Peeters, 2014). Note also another title: Gary Dorrien, *The Word as True Myth: Interpreting Modern Theology* (Louisville, KY: Westminster John Knox Press, 1997).
44. See William K. Ferrell, *Literature and Film as Modern Myth* (Westport, CT: Praeger, 2000).
45. C. S. Lewis, *The Lion, the Witch, and the Wardrobe* (New York: Macmillan, 1950), 149.
46. Rudolf Otto, *The Idea of the Holy*, trans. John W. Harvey (New York: Oxford University Press, 1958).
47. Robert J. Fogelin, *Figuratively Speaking* (New Haven: Yale University Press, 1988), 4.

Chapter 2

1. Andrew C. Scott, *Fire: A Very Short Introduction* (New York: Oxford University Press, 2020), 53.
2. Grace Nichols, "Caribbean Woman Prayer," *A Treasury of Christian Poetry: 700 Inspiring and Beloved Poems*, com. Mary Batchelor (New York: Gramercy Books, 1995), 387.
3. Romanos, "On the Holy Theophany," trans. Ephrem Lash, *On the Life of Christ* (San Francisco: HarperCollins, 1995), 42.

4. Thanks to Avivah Gottlieb Zornberg for this reference: "Golden Calf and consuming fire," *The Christian Century*, December 2022, 81.
5. Norman Nicholson, "The Burning Bush," *A Treasury of Christian Poetry: 700 Inspiring and Beloved Poems*, 515.
6. Hildegard of Bingen, *Scivias*, trans. Mother Columba Hart and Jane Bishop (New York: Paulist, 1990), 163–164.
7. For a proposal that "first" and "second" testaments is preferable terminology, see Gail Ramshaw, "The First Testament within Christian Lectionaries," *Worship* 64 (1990): 494–510.
8. Cited in Bogdan Bucur, *Scriptures Re-envisioned: Christophanic Exegesis and the Making of a Christian Bible* (Leiden: Brill, 2019), 171.
9. See for example the Old Testament depictions of God as Christ in *Bible Moralisée*, Codex 2554, edited by Gerald B. Guest (London: Harvey Miller Publishers, 1995).
10. Bucur, *Scriptures Re-envisioned*, 4–5.
11. Bucur, chapter 1 on Luke 24, *Scriptures Re-envisioned*, 5–41.
12. *The Prayers of Catherine of Siena*, ed. Suzanne Noffke OP (New York: Paulist, 1983), 104, 186.
13. Bucur, *Scriptures Re-envisioned*, 110–118.
14. Bucur, *Scriptures Re-envisioned*, 258–259.
15. *Quodvultdeus of Carthage: The Creedal Homilies*, trans. Thomas Macy Finn (New York: Newman Press, 2004), 63.
16. Gertrude of Helfta, *The Herald of Divine Love*, 105.
17. The text of the Exultet is cited from *Evangelical Lutheran Worship, Leaders Desk Edition* (Minneapolis: Augsburg Fortress, 2006), 646–647.
18. D. Elton Trueblood, "God, Whose Purpose Is to Kindle," *Voices Together*, #152.

Chapter 3

1. See Irene Nowell, *Sing a New Song: The Psalms in the Sunday Lectionary* (Collegeville, MN: Liturgical Press, 1993); and

Ramshaw, *Word of God, Word of Life*, 67–80, for discussions of the Sunday psalms.

2. *The Confessions of St. Augustine*, Book 10: 27, trans. John K. Ryan (New York: Doubleday, 1960), 254.
3. See Alison Reith Gray, *Psalm 18 in Words and Pictures: A Reading through Metaphor* (Leiden: Brill, 2014), for a thorough analysis of Psalm 18.
4. Thomas Troeger, "Source and Sovereign, Rock and Cloud," *All Creation Sings* (Minneapolis: Augsburg Fortress, 2020), #947.
5. "The Passion of Saints Perpetua and Felicity," *Mystics, Visionaries, and Prophets: A Historical Anthology of Women's Spiritual Writings*, ed. Shawn Madigan (Minneapolis: Fortress Press, 1998), 16.
6. Mechthild of Magdeburg, *The Flowing Light of the Godhead*, trans. Frank Tobin (New York: Paulist Press, 1998), 45–46.
7. Julian of Norwich, "A Revelation of Love," *The Writings of Julian of Norwich*, ed. Nicholas Watson and Jacqueline Jenkins (University Park, PA: The Pennsylvania State University, 2006), 195.
8. Herbert F. Brokering, "Thine the Amen," *Evangelical Lutheran Worship* (Minneapolis: Augsburg Fortress, 2006), #826.
9. R. Kendall Soulen, *Irrevocable: The Name of God and the Unity of the Christian Bible* (Minneapolis: Fortress Press, 2022) argues that the tetragrammaton, the holiest name of God, ought to function among Christians as the preferred name of the triune God.
10. Anonymous, "Be Thou My Vision," *Evangelical Lutheran Worship*, #793.
11. See Francesca Stavrakopoulou, *God: An Anatomy* (New York: Knopf, 2021), in which all the biblical passages that cite parts of the body of God are discussed. Stavrakopoulou rejects any and all metaphoric interpretations, in the past or the present, of such biblical speech, and thus claims that the biblical God is no longer worshiped.
12. See Halton, *A Human-Shaped God.*

13. John Thornburg, "God the Sculptor of the Mountain," *Evangelical Lutheran Worship*, # 736.
14. Augustus M. Toplady, "Rock of Ages," *Evangelical Lutheran Worship*, #623.
15. Soskice, *Naming God,* 58.
16. See Arthur I. Waskow, *Seasons of Our Joy: A Handbook of Jewish Festivals* (New York: Summit Books, 1982), xvi.
17. Nicola Slee, *Abba, Amma: Improvisations on the Lord's Prayer* (Norwich: Canterbury Press, 2022).
18. Julian of Norwich, *A Revelation of Love*, 135.
19. See for example the board book by Carol Wehrheim, *The Loving Shepherd* (Cleveland: United Church Press, 1997).
20. For various opinions about Wisdom, see for example Roland E. Murphy, *The Tree of Life: An Exploration of Biblical Wisdom Literature*, 3rd ed. (Grand Rapids: Eerdmans, 1990); Elizabeth A. Johnson, *She Who Is: The Mystery of God in Feminist Theological Discourse* (New York: Crossroad, 1992), 124–187; and Susan Cady, Marian Ronan, and Hal Taussig, *Sophia: The Future of Feminist Spirituality* (San Francisco: Harper & Row, 1986).
21. Denise Levertov, "In Whom We Live and Move and Have Our Being," *Sands of the Well* (New York: New Directions, 1994), 107.
22. John Ryan, *The Hymns of Ann Griffiths*, trans. Robert O. F. Wynne (Caernarfon, Wales: Ty Ar y Graig, 1980), 113.
23. Donne, "prayer 1," *Devotions Upon Emergent Occasions*, 25.
24. *Pseudo-Dionysius: The Complete Works*, trans. Colm Luibheid (New York: Paulist Press, 1987), 263.
25. Miriam Therese Winter, *Woman Prayer Woman Song: Resources for Ritual*, illus. Meinrad Craighead (New York: Crossroad, 1990), 215.
26. "I Am That Great and Fiery Force," *Voices Together*, #663.
27. *Early Christian Prayers*, ed. A. Hamman OFM, trans. Walter Mitchell (n.p.: St. Pius X Press, n.d.), 64.
28. Paul Tillich, *Systematic Theology*, vol. 1 (Chicago: University of Chicago Press, 1952), 235–236.

29. Frances Minkoff, "O Healing River," *Voices Together*, #706.
30. Martin J. Nystrom, "As the Deer," *Glory to God: The Presbyterian Hymnal* (Louisville: Westminster John Knox Press, 2013), #626.
31. William Wordsworth, "Ode: Intimations of Immortality from Recollections of Early Childhood," www.poetryfoundation.org/poems/45536 (accessed February 1, 2024).
32. Boethius, trans. M. Counsell, *2000 Years of Prayer*, ed. Michael Counsell (Harrisburg, PA: Morehouse Publishing, 1999), 36.
33. Francis Quarles, "The Loadstone," www.allpoetry.com/The-Loadstone (accessed January 29, 2024).
34. Rend Collective, "My Lighthouse," *Voices Together*, #597.
35. Romano Guardini, *Prayers from Theology*, trans. Richard Newnham (New York: Herder and Herder, 1962), 23.
36. Columba, *2000 Years of Prayer*, 77.
37. John Mason, "How shall I sing that majesty," *2000 Years of Prayer*, 297.
38. Dan Damon, "Shadow and Substance," *The New Century Hymnal* (Cleveland, OH: Pilgrim Press, 1995), #398.
39. Joseph R. Renville, "Wakantanki taku nitawa," trans. Philip Frazier as "Many and Great, O God," *Evangelical Lutheran Worship*, #837.
40. Correspondence with Rev. Dr. Stephen Burns, reporting on *A Prayer Book for Australia*.
41. Johann Scheffler, "Thee Will I Love, My Strength, My Tower," *Lutheran Book of Worship* (Minneapolis: Augsburg Publishing House, 1978), #502.
42. John of the Cross, "O Living Flame of Love," *The Poems of St. John of the Cross* (New York: New Directions, 1972), 57.
43. *The Prayers of Peter Marshall*, ed. Catherine Marshall (New York: McGraw-Hill Book Company, 1949), 140.
44. "O Mighty Author of the world," in *The Divine Office Hymnal* (Chicago: GIA Publications, 2023), #213.
45. Alla Renée Bozarth, *Womanpriest: A Personal Odyssey*, rev. ed. (San Diego: LuraMedia, 1988), 166.

46. Christena Cleveland, *God is a Black Woman* (New York: HarperOne, 2022).
47. Ted Loder, "I Am So Thankful to Be Alive," *Guerrillas of Grace: Prayers for the Battle* (Minneapolis: Augsburg Books, 1981), 46.
48. John G. Neihardt, *Black Elk Speaks* (New York: William Morrow and Company, 1932), 5.
49. David Adam, *The Edge of Glory: Prayers in the Celtic Tradition* (London: Triangle, 1985), 13.
50. Timothy J. Mark, in *The Westminster Collection of Christian Prayers*, compiled by Dorothy M. Stewart (Louisville: Westminster John Knox Press, 2002), 366.
51. Catherine of Siena, *The Dialogue*, trans. Suzanne Noffke OP (New York: Paulist Press, 1980), 325.
52. Anonymous, "God, our Father and our Mother," *A Shaker Hymnal: A Facsimile Edition of the 1908 Hymnal of the Canterbury Shakers* (Woodstock, NH: Overlook Press, 1990), 30.
53. *Anglican Eucharistic Liturgies 1985–2010*, ed. Colin Buchanan (London: Canterbury Press, 2011), 149.
54. Dimitri of Rostov, in Bishop Kallistos Ware, *The Orthodox Way* (Crestwood, NY: St. Vladimir's Seminary Press, 1993), 21.
55. Alfred, Lord Tennyson, "Crossing the Bar," www.poetryfoundation.org/poems/45321 (accessed February 1, 2024).
56. John Milton, Sonnet 7, "How Soon hath Time, the subtle thief of youth," www.poetryfoundation.org/poems/44744 (accessed February 1, 2024).
57. Charles Wesley, "Wrestling Jacob," in *2000 Years of Prayer*, 316.
58. William Whitla, "Let Streams of Living Justice," *Evangelical Lutheran Worship*, #710.
59. Harris J. Loewen, "O God, Great Womb," *Voices Together*, #176.
60. Wren, "Bring Many Names," *What Language Shall I Borrow? God-Talk in Worship, A Male Responds to Feminist Theology* (New York: Crossroad, 1989), 152.
61. Janet Martin Soskice, *The Kindness of God: Metaphor, Gender, and Religious Language* (New York: Oxford University Press, 2007), 5 and passim.

62. Dhuoda of Septimania, *Mystics, Visionaries, and Prophets*, 84, 86.
63. Wren, "Bring Many Names," *What Language Shall I Borrow*, 138.
64. Jane Parker Huber, "God, Creation's Great Designer," *The New Century Hymnal*, #371.
65. See Jennifer L. Lord, *Finding Language and Imagery: Words for Holy Speech* (Minneapolis: Fortress Press, 2010), 17–26. For a listing of the images in the readings of the three-year lectionaries, see Ramshaw, *Treasures Old and New: Images in the Lectionary* (Minneapolis: Augsburg Fortress, 2002), 438–451.

Chapter 4

1. John Newton, "How Sweet the Name of Jesus Sounds," *Evangelical Lutheran Worship*, #620.
2. See for example *Homilies for the Christian People, Cycles A, B. C*, ed. Gail Ramshaw (New York: Pueblo Publishing Company, 1989), 194–196.
3. See the Greek Orthodox icon of Saint Anna the Prophetess by AgioErgo, accessed on February 14, 2024 on www.etsy.com/your/shops/AgioErgo.
4. Anonymous, "Away in a manger," *Evangelical Lutheran Worship*, #277.
5. Marcus Aurelius Clemens Prudentius, "Of the Father's Love Begotten," *Evangelical Lutheran Worship*, #295.
6. For more thorough explications of these figures of speech, see the magisterial work of my seminary professor Raymond E. Brown SS, *The Gospel according to John,* volume 1 and 2, The Anchor Bible 29 and 29A (Garden City, NY: Doubleday & Company, 1966 and 1970).
7. Chaim Potok, *My Name is Asher Lev* (New York: Fawcett Crest, 1972), 163.

8. A helpful guide to the language of "Son of God" is Christopher Bryan's *Son of God: Reflections on a Tradition* (New York: Oxford University Press, 2023).
9. James Quinn, "Word of God, Come Down on Earth," *Evangelical Lutheran Worship*, #510.
10. Anonymous, "What Wondrous Love is This," *Evangelical Lutheran Worship*, #666.
11. Anonymous, "Methinks I see," www.hymnary.org/text/methinks_i_see_an_heavenly_host.
12. For more details, see Gail Ramshaw, *God beyond Gender*, 47–58.
13. See Pauline Matarasso, *Clothed in Language* (Collegeville, MN: Liturgical Press, 2019), 88.
14. Anonymous, trans. John Mason Neale, "O Come, O Come, Emmanuel," *Evangelical Lutheran Worship*, #257.
15. Patrick Michaels, "Who Comes from God," *Voices United* (Etobicoke, CA: The United Church Publishing House, 1996), #892.
16. Moises B. Andrade, "When Twilight Comes," *Evangelical Lutheran Worship*, #566.
17. Philipp Nicolai, "O Morning Star," *Evangelical Lutheran Worship*, #308.
18. Augustine, cited in Louis Charbonneau-Lassay, *The Bestiary of Christ*, trans. and abr. F. M. Dooling (New York: Parabola Books, 1991), 8.
19. For an extensive discussion of animal images of Christ, see Louis Charbonneau-Lassay, *The Bestiary of Christ.*
20. Tertullian, in Lawrence J. Johnson, ed., *Worship in the Early Church: An Anthology of Historical Sources*, vol. 1 (Collegeville, MN: Liturgical Press, 2009), 119.
21. See for example He Qi, "Supper at Emmaus," *Evangelical Lutheran Worship*, 89.
22. C. S. Lewis, *The Lion, the Witch and the Wardrobe*, 131–134.
23. Thomas Aquinas, "Thee We Adore, O Hidden Savior," *Lutheran Service Book* (St. Louis: Concordia Publishing House, 2006), #640.

24. Aaron Koch, "Jesus, Our Scapegoat," www.mountziongreenfield.org/sermons/jesus-is-ous-scapegoat.
25. See "The Unicorn," in *The Bestiary of Christ*, 369.
26. Jim Cotter, last stanza, "Expectant: verses for Advent," *Cairns Publications* (London: Canterbury Press, 2002).
27. Gertrude Morgan, "Jesus is my air Plane," Smithsonian American Art Museum, www.Americanart.si.edu/artwork/Jesus-is-my-airplane 17913.
28. Niceta of Remesiana, "The Names and Titles of Our Saviour," *Writings*, trans. Gerald G. Walsh (New York: The Fathers of the Church, Inc., 1949), 11–12.
29. *The Book of Margery Kempe*, trans. B. A. Windeatt (New York: Penguin Books, 1985), 114.
30. See for example Elizabeth Alvilda Petroff, "Introduction," *Medieval Women's Visionary Literature* (New York: Oxford University Press, 1986), 3–59.
31. Johann Franck, "Soul, Adorn Yourself with Gladness," *Evangelical Lutheran Worship*, #488.
32. Jacopone da Todi, in *2000 Years of Prayer*, 147.
33. Richard Hutchins, "Christ the Appletree," www.hymnary.org.
34. Eusebius, *Ecclesiastical History*, trans. Kirsopp Lake, vol. 1 (Cambridge, MA: Harvard University Press, 1926), 427.
35. "The Dream of the Rood," trans. Roy Liuzza, www.poetryfoundation/poems/159129.
36. Catherine of Siena, *The Dialogue*, 64–160.
37. Matthäus Apelles von Loewenstern, "Jesus, our Captain," www.hymnary.org.
38. Richard Leach, "O Carpenter, Why Leave the Bench," *Glory to God*, #162.
39. Clement of Alexandria, "Prayer to the Divine Tutor," ed. A. Hamman OFM, *Early Christian Prayers* (n.p.: St. Pius X Press, n.d.), 39.
40. Julian of Norwich, *A Revelation of Love*, 139.

41. Herbert Brokering, "Alleluia! Jesus Is Risen," *Evangelical Lutheran Worship*, #377.
42. Philipp Nicolai, "O Morning Star," *Evangelical Lutheran Worship*, #308.
43. "O Come, O Come, Emmanuel," *Evangelical Lutheran Worship*, #257.
44. Charles Wesley, "O Thou Eternal Victim Slain," www.hymnary.org.
45. Janet Morley, *All Desires Known*, expanded ed. (London: SPCK 1992), 13.
46. Sylvia Dunstan, "You, Lord, Are Both Lamb and Shepherd," *All Creation Sings*, #954.
47. George Herbert, "Come, My Way, My Truth, My Life," *Evangelical Lutheran Worship*, #816.
48. Fred Kaan, "We Meet You, O Christ," *Voices United,* #183.
49. Jehioada Brewer, "Hail, sovereign love," www.hymnary.org.
50. See for example Elizabeth Jennings, "A Christmas Sequence," *A Treasury of Christian Poetry*, 281.
51. "O Come, O Come, Emmanuel," *Evangelical Lutheran Worship*, #257.
52. Gwendolyn R. Henry, *Falling in Love with Jesus, My Knight in Shining Armor* (n.p.: Get Published Successfully, 2019).
53. "Prayers from Papyri and Potsherds," *Early Christian Prayers*, 74.
54. Charles A. Tindley, "When the Storms of Life Are Raging," *Voices Together*, #595.
55. Lillian W. Cassaday, "O Christians, Leagued Together," *Service Book and Hymnal* (Minneapolis: Augsburg Publishing House, 1958), #567.
56. John Mason, "I've found the pearl of greatest price," www.hymnary.org.
57. Martin Luther, "Dear Christians, One and All, Rejoice," *Evangelical Lutheran Worship*, #594.
58. See Gustaf Aulén, *Christus Victor: An Historical Study of the Three Main Types of the Idea of the Atonement*, trans. A. G. Hebert (New York: Macmillan, 1969), 49–57.

59. J. Andrew Fowler, "The Rice of Life," *All Creation Sings*, #965.
60. Anonymous, "Lo, How a Rose E'er Blooming," *Evangelical Lutheran Worship*, #272.
61. Les Petites Soeurs de Jésus and L'Arche Community, "Lord Jesus, You Shall Be My Song," *Evangelical Lutheran Worship*, #808.
62. Herman Stuempfle, Jr., "A Sower Came from Ancient Hills," *Glory to God*, #171
63. Christopher Smart, "Where Is This Stupendous Stranger," *Voices Together*, #266.
64. Johann Franck, "Jesus, Priceless Treasure," *Evangelical Lutheran Worship*, #775.
65. See William P. Brown, *Seeing the Psalms*, 55–79.
66. Venantius Honorius Fortunatus, "Sing, My Tongue," *Evangelical Lutheran Worship*, # 355 or 356, and "The Royal Banners Forward Go," *Lutheran Service Book*, #455. See also Christopher Irvine, *The Cross and Creation in Christian Liturgy and Art* (Collegeville, MN: Liturgical Press, 2013), 170–204; and Frances M. Young, *Constructing the Cross: Type, Sign, Symbol, Word, Action* (Eugene, OR: Cascade Books, 2015), 44–72.
67. Pécselyi Király Imre, "There in God's Garden," *Evangelical Lutheran Worship*, #342.
68. *The Orthodox Study Bible* (Nashville: Thomas Nelson, 2008), 1747.
69. See Marty Haugen, "Tree of Life and Awesome Mystery" and Susan Palo Cherwien, "O Blessed Spring," *Evangelical Lutheran Worship*, #334 and 447.
70. Alan Gaunt, "Translations from the Welsh of Ann Griffiths," *Always from Joy* (London: Stainer & Bell, 1997), 93.
71. Brian Wren, "Will God Be Judge?" *New Beginnings* (Carol Stream, IL: Hope Publishing Company, 1993), #21.
72. Martin Luther, sermon on the annunciation, *The Martin Luther Christmas Book*, trans. and ed. Roland H. Bainton (Philadelphia: Muhlenberg Press, 1958), 23.
73. In "Holy Communion, setting 12," *All Creation Sings*, 41.

74. Pope Damasus, in Lucien Deiss CSSP, *Springtime of the Liturgy: Liturgical Texts of the First Four Centuries,* trans. Matthew J. O'Connell (Collegeville, Minnesota: Liturgical Press, 1967), 258–259.
75. John Macquarrie, *God-Talk: An Examination of the Language and Logic of Theology* (New York: Seabury Press, 1979, 212–230.
76. A. S. Byatt, *The Children's Book* (New York: Random House, 2009), 162.
77. See Isaac S.Villegas, "Son of Man . . . Vindicated by Her Deeds," *Worship* 97 (2023), 160–175, for a plea for the alternation of gendered pronouns for Christ.
78. Michael Frye, "Jesus, Be the Center," *Voices Together*, #584.
79. See "Good Friday," *Evangelical Lutheran Worship, Leaders Edition*, 634–642.

Chapter 5

1. Delores Dufner OSB, "O Spirit All-Embracing," *All Creation Sings*, #944.
2. See Charles Halton for the opposite opinion.
3. Cited in Sebastian Brock, *Fire from Heaven: Studies in Syriac Theology and Liturgy* (Burlington, VT: Ashgate Publishing Company, 2006), 255.
4. See for example the little book by Sally Hines, *Is Gender Fluid? A Primer for the 21st Century* (London: Thames & Hudson, 2018).
5. Doris Akers, "Sweet, Sweet Spirit," *Lead Me, Guide Me: The African American Catholic Hymnal* (Chicago: GIA Publications, 1987), #75.
6. James K. Manley, "Spirit of Gentleness," *Evangelical Lutheran Worship*, #396.
7. Herman G. Stuempfle, "God of Tempest, God of Whirlwind," *Evangelical Lutheran Worship*, #400.
8. Etienne Vetö, *The Breath of God: An Essay on the Holy Spirit in the Trinity* (Eugene, OR: Cascade Books, 2019).

9. Osvaldo Catena, "O Living Breath of God," *Evangelical Lutheran Worship*, #407.
10. T. S. Eliot, "Little Gidding," *The Complete Poems and Plays 1909–1950* (New York: Harcourt, Brace & World, 1958), 143.
11. See for example "My Soul Proclaims Your Greatness," *Evangelical Lutheran Worship*, #251.
12. Ambrose, "The Holy Spirit," ch. 20, *Saint Ambrose: Theological and Dogmatic Works*, trans. Roy J. Deferrari (Washington, DC: Catholic University of America Press, 1963), 209.
13. Of the many available translations and emendations of *Veni Creator Spiritus*, the one cited in Wikipedia is Edward Caswall's 1849 version in *The Lutheran Hymnal* (Saint Louis: Concordia Publishing House, 1941), #233.
14. Victoria Walton, in *2000 Years of Prayer*, 516–517.
15. A close translation of *Veni Sancte Spiritus* is titled "Pentecost Sequence," in *Glory & Praise*, 3rd ed. (Portland, OR: OCP, 2015), #349.
16. Symeon the New Theologian, "Mystical Prayer," *Hymns of Divine Love*, trans. George A. Maloney (Denville, NJ: Dimension Books, n.d.), 9.
17. Hildegard of Bingen, "Sequence for the Holy Spirit," *Saint Hildegard of Bingen: Symphonia*, trans. Barbara Newman (Ithaca: Cornell University Press, 1988), 149.
18. Merlin Carothers, *Prison to Praise* (Escondido, CA.: Merlin R. Carothers, 1970), 79.
19. Ruth Duck, "Moved by the Gospel, Let Us Move," *Voices United*, #394.
20. "There Is a Balm in Gilead," *Evangelical Lutheran Worship*, #614.
21. Catherine of Siena, *The Dialogue*, 335.
22. Jean Janzen, "O Holy Spirit, Root of Life," *Evangelical Lutheran Worship*, #399.
23. Charles Wesley, "Captain of Israel's host," *Together in Song: Australian Hymn Book II* (Sydney, Australia: HarperCollins Publishers, 1999), #574.
24. Jody L. Caldwell, "O Fiery Spirit," *Voices Together*, #55.

25. Edmund Rybarczyk, *The Spirit Unfettered: Protestant Views on the Holy Spirit* (Brewster, MA: Paraclete Press, 2010), 89.
26. John B. Geyer, "We Know That Christ Is Raised," *Evangelical Lutheran Worship*, #449.
27. Madeleine Forell Marshall, "Sweet Delight, Most Lovely," *The New Century Hymnal*, #269.
28. Michael Schirmer, "O Holy Ghost, Descend We Pray," www.hymnary.org.
29. Shirley Erena Murray, "Spirit of Love," *The New Century Hymnal*, #58.
30. Shirley Erena Murray, "Loving Spirit," *Evangelical Lutheran Worship*, #397.
31. Tom Colvin, "God Sends Us His Spirit," *Lead Me, Guide Me: The African American Catholic Hymnal*, #125.
32. Irenaeus, "Against Heresies," vol. 1, *The Ante-Nicene Fathers*, ed. Alexander Roberts and James Donaldson (Grand Rapids, MI: W. B. Eerdmans, 1969), 487–488.
33. Marty Haugen, "Healer of Our Every Ill," *Evangelical Lutheran Worship*, #612.
34. Toyohiko Kagawa, *Meditations on the Holy Spirit*, trans. Charles A. Logan (Nashville: Cokesbury Press, 1939), 165.
35. John L. Bell and Graham Maule, "She Sits Like a Bird," *Together in Song*, #418.
36. "Ash Wednesday," *Evangelical Lutheran Worship*, 253.
37. Evening Liturgy A, The Wild Goose Worship Group, *A Wee Worship Book*, 4th ed. (Chicago: GIA Publications, 1999), 54.
38. Josua Stegmann, "Come, Rain from the heavens," www.hymnary.org.
39. Michael Schirmer, "O Holy Spirit, Enter In," *Evangelical Lutheran Worship*, #786.
40. Hildegard of Bingen, "Antiphon for the Holy Spirit," in Barbara Newman, 2nd ed., *Saint Hildegard of Bingen: Symphonia*, 140–141.
41. Ignatius of Antioch, "Epistle to the Ephesians," paragraph 9, *Early Christian Fathers*, 90.

42. Leonardo Boff, *Come, Holy Spirit: Inner Fire, Giver of Life & Comforter of the Poor*, trans. Margaret Wilde (Maryknoll, NY: Orbis Books, 2015), 195.
43. Ambrose, "The Holy Spirit," *Theological and Dogmatic Works*, 169.
44. Symeon the New Theologian, *Hymns of Divine Love*, 239.
45. Ray Simpson, *A Holy Island Prayer Book: Morning, Midday and Evening Prayer* (Norwich: Canterbury Press, 2002), 77.
46. Brian Wren, "Holy Spirit, storm of love," *What Language Shall I Borrow*, 204. Also in *Common Praise* (Toronto: Anglican Book Centre, 1998), #603.
47. Hymns on the Nativity 5, *Ephrem the Syrian Hymns*, trans. Kathleen E. McVey (New York: Paulist Press, 1989), 107.
48. Mary H. Streufert, *Language for God: A Lutheran Perspective* (Minneapolis: Fortress Press, 2022), 8.
49. Flannery O'Connor, *The Habit of Being: The Letters of Flannery O'Connor*, ed. Sally Fitzgerald (New York: Vintage Books, 1980), 354.
50. Hildegard of Bingen, "Sequence for the Holy Spirit," in Elizabeth Dreyer, *Holy Power, Holy Presence: Rediscovering Medieval Metaphors for the Holy Spirit* (New York: Paulist Press, 2007), 81–82.

Chapter 6

1. Symeon the New Theologian, *Hymns of Divine Love*, 233–234.
2. See for example Robert W. Jenson, *The Triune Identity: God According to the Gospel.*
3. See for example Catherine Mowry LaCugna, *God For Us: The Trinity and Christian Life* (San Francisco: Harper, 1991).
4. Karl Barth, *Church Dogmatics: The Doctrine of the Word of God*, vol. I, part 1, trans. G. W. Bromiley, ed. G. W. Bromiley and T. F. Torrance (London: T & T Clark, 2004), 120–121.
5. Brian Wren, *Bring Many Names*, #22.

6. See Jane Schaberg, *The Father, the Son and the Holy Spirit: The Triadic Phrase in Matthew 28:19b,* Dissertation Series 61 (Chico, CA: Scholars Press, 1982).
7. Robert W. Jenson, *Systematic Theology: The Triune God,* vol. 1 (New York: Oxford University Press, 1997), 46.
8. Julia A. J. Foote, "A Brand Plucked from the Fire," in Susan Houchins, ed., *Spiritual Narratives* (New York: Oxford University Press, 1988), 109.
9. Alternative Blessings, *A New Zealand Prayer Book* (Auckland: William Collins Publishers, 1989), 545. See also Gail Ramshaw, "Naming the Trinity: Orthodoxy and Inclusivity," *Worship* 60 (1986): 491–498.
10. Ruth Duck, *Gender and the Name of God: The Trinitarian Baptismal Formula* (New York: Pilgrim Press, 1991), 163.
11. Bryan Cones, "Orthodoxy *and* Inclusivity: Naming God in Baptism," in *Conversations about Divine Mystery: Essays in Honor of Gail Ramshaw,* ed. Stephen Burns and HyeRan Kim-Cragg (Minneapolis: Fortress Press, 2023), 63–65.
12. Michael Downey, *Altogether Gift: A Trinitarian Spirituality* (Maryknoll, NY: Orbis Books, 2000), 58–59.
13. *The Works of Bernard of Clairvaux,* sermon 8, 2.7, vol. 2, "On the Song of Songs" I, trans. Kilian Walsh OSCO (Spencer, MA: Cistercian Publications, 1971), 47, 51.
14. "The Cup of Milk," *The Earliest Christian Hymnbook: The Odes of Solomon,* trans. James H. Charlesworth (Eugene, OR: Cascade Books, 2009).
15. Augustine, *The Trinity,* trans. Stephen McKenna (Washington, DC: Catholic University of America Press, 2017), book 8.10, 266.
16. Peter W. A. Davison, "When Long Before Time: The Singer and the Song," *Evangelical Lutheran Worship,* #861.
17. Michael Edward Hewlett, "Praise the Spirit in creation," *Together in Song,* #415.
18. Marguerite Porete, *The Mirror of Simple Souls,* trans. Ellen L. Babinsky (New York: Paulist, 1993), 185.

19. Mechthild of Magdeburg, *The Flowing Light of the Godhead*, 186.
20. Southern Africa Synod of Bishops 22005–2008, First Eucharistic Prayer for Season of Creation, *Anglican Eucharistic Liturgies 1985–2020*, ed. Colin Buchanan (London: Canterbury Press, 2011), 171.
21. See for example Ruth C. Duck, *Gender and the Name of God*, 171–172.
22. Anne Hunt, *The Trinity: Insights from the Mystics* (Collegeville, MN: Liturgical Press, 2010), 153.
23. Ben Jonson, "To Heaven," *2000 Years of Prayer*, 238–239.
24. Walter Brueggemann, "Work your wonders," *Awed to Heaven, Rooted in Earth* (Minneapolis: Fortress Press, 2003), 117.
25. Julian of Norwich, *A Revelation of Love*, 309–311.
26. *Uniting in Worship 2* (Sydney: Uniting Church Press, 2005), 198.
27. Augustine, *The Trinity*, book 15.23, 509–510.
28. Ruth Duck, "Womb of Life and Source of Being," *All Creation Sings*, #948.
29. Bobby McFerrin, "The 23rd Psalm lyrics," www.lyricsfreak.com.
30. Sallie McFague, *Models of God: Theology for an Ecological, Nuclear Age* (Philadelphia: Fortress Press, 1987).
31. *The Prayers of Catherine of Siena*, 102.
32. Francis of Assisi, in *2000 Years of Prayer*, 142.
33. *Uniting in Worship* (Sydney, Australia: Assembly of the Uniting Church in Australia, 2005), 224.
34. Worship Texts for November, *Sundays and Seasons Year B 2024* (Minneapolis: Augsburg Fortress, 2023), 290.
35. Karl Barth, cited in R. Kendall Soulen, *The Divine Name(s) and the Holy Trinity*, 94.
36. Richard Leach, "Come, Join the Dance of Trinity," *Evangelical Lutheran Worship*, #412.
37. Mary Kathleen Speegle Schmitt, *Seasons of the Feminine Divine: Christian Feminist Prayers for the Liturgical Cycle* (New York: Crossroad, 1993), 85.

38. Dante, *The Divine Comedy: Paradise*, xxxiii: 115–120, trans. Mark Musa (New York: Penguin, 1984), 393.
39. Quodvultdeus, *The Creedal Homilies*, 63.
40. Gertrude of Helfta, *The Herald of Divine Love*, 176.
41. Robert W. Jenson, *Systematic Theology*, vol. 1, 236.
42. Hildegard of Bingen, *Homilies on the Gospels*, trans. Beverly Mayne Kienzle, homilies 19 and 26 (Collegeville, MI: Liturgical Press, 2011), 92, 120.
43. Elisabeth of Schönau, Second Book of Visions 4, trans. Anne L Clark, *Elisabeth of Schönau: The Complete Works* (New York: Paulist Press, 2000), 98–99.
44. Tertullian, "Praxeas" 8, in Robert Letham, *The Holy Trinity: In Scripture, History, Theology, and Worship* (Phillipsburg, NJ: P & R Publishing Company, 2004), 101.
45. John of Damascus, Treatise 1.11, *Three Treatises on the Divine Images*, 26.
46. Thanksgiving at the Font C, *All Creation Sings*, 60.
47. David S. Cunningham, *These Three Are One: The Practice of Trinitarian Theology* (Malden, MA: Blackwell Publishers, 1998).
48. Elizabeth A. Johnson, *She Who Is*.
49. *The Prayers of Catherine of Siena*, 147–153.
50. For a list compiled in 2010 of some ninety examples of the "unfolding of the name of the Trinity," see R. Kendall Soulen, *Divine Names(s) and the Holy Trinity*, 248–251.
51. *The Hélène Cixous Reader*, ed. Susan Sellers (New York: Routledge, 1994), 8, xvii–xviii.
52. Anne Hunt, *Trinity: Nexis of the Mysteries of Christian Faith* (Maryknoll, NY: Orbis, 2005), 227.
53. Carmen Renee Berry, *The Unathorized Guide to Choosing a Church* (Grand Rapids: Brazos Press, 2003), 56–60 and throughout.
54. Litany for Trinity Sunday, *Book of Common Worship* (Louisville: Westminster John Knox Press, 2018), 353–354.
55. Mary Kathleen Speegle Schmitt, *Seasons of the Feminine Divine*, 46, 59, 72, 73, 81–82, 106–107, 120.

56. Ruth C. Duck and Patricia Wilson-Kastner, *Praising God: The Trinity in Christian Worship* (Louisville: Westminster John Knox Press, 1999), 141–142.
57. "Praise God (Doxology)," *Voices Together*, #71.
58. Julian of Norwich, *The Revelations of Love*, 275–277.
59. Angela of Foligno, "The Book of Blessed Angela," in *Angela of Foligno: Complete Works*, trans. Paul Lachance OFM (New York: Paulist Press, 1993), 145.

Chapter 7

1. John Polkinghorne, *Science and the Trinity: The Christian Encounter with Reality* (New Haven, CT: Yale University Press, 2004), xiii.
2. "Sweet Lord," Cesáreo Gabaráin, trans. Madeleine Forell Marshall, "You Have Come Down to the Lakeshore," *Evangelical Lutheran Worship*, #817.
3. *The Book of Margery Kempe*, trans. B. A. Windeatt, 75.
4. Ephrem the Syrian, in Sidney H. Griffith, *Faith Adoring the Mystery: Reading the Bible with St Ephraem the Syrian* (Milwaukee, WI: Marquette University Press, 1997), 26.
5. Gabrielle Bossis, *He and I*, cited in *Mystics, Visionaries and Prophets: A Historical Anthology of Women's Spiritual Writings*, ed. Shawn Madigan (Minneapolis: Fortress Press, 1998), 334.
6. Several of the best examples of Christian discussion of myth are Thomas Fawcett, *Hebrew Myth and Christian Gospel*; Paul K.-K. Cho, *Myth, History, and Metaphor in the Hebrew Bible* (New York: Cambridge University Press, 2019); Burton Mack, *The Christian Myth: Origins, Logic, and Legacy* (New York: Continuum, 2001); and Gary Dorrien, *The Word as True Myth: Interpreting Modern Theology*.
7. Stephen P. Starke, "Water, Blood, and Spirit Crying," *Lutheran Service Book*, #597.

8. A thorough anthology of creation myths is Barbara C. Sprout, *Primal Myths: Creation Myths Around the World* (New York: HarperCollins, 1979).
9. See for example David Adams Leeming, *The World of Myth: An Anthology* (New York: Oxford University Press, 1990), 32–62.
10. Cited in James G. Frazer, *The Great Flood: A Handbook of World Flood Myths* (Albany, NY: JasonColavita.com Books, 2013), 45–46.
11. See for example Henry M. Morris and Martin E. Clark, *The Bible Has the Answer*, 100–110.
12. Ambrose, "The Mysteries," 3.10, trans. Roy J. Deferrari, *Saint Ambrose: Theological and Dogmatic Works* (Washington, DC: Catholic University of America Press, 1963), 8.
13. Harry Emerson Fosdick, "What is the Matter with Preaching," *Harpers Magazine*, vol. 157 (July 1928): 135.
14. Carmel McCarthy, *Saint Ephrem's Commentary on Tatian's Diatessaron* (Oxford: Oxford University Press, 1993), 49–50.
15. See for example Thomas Fawcett, "The Nativity Stories," *Hebrew Myth and Christian Gospel*, 138–148, and David Adams Leeming, "The Conception, Birth, and Childhood of the Hero," in *The World of Myth*, 221–235.
16. Hugo Rahner and Karl Rahner, *Prayers for Meditation* (New York: Herder & Herder, 1962), 12.
17. Symeon the New Theologian, *Hymns of Divine Love*, 27.
18. *The Cloud of Unknowing*, ch. 73, trans. William Johnston (Garden City, NY: Doubleday & Company, 1973), 142; *Cloud of Unknowing*, ch. 65, 132.
19. The appendices in *Treasures Old and New* provide lists of the images contained in each Sunday's lectionary readings, 438–451.
20. Paul Ricoeur, *The Rule of Metaphor*, 24.
21. Roy A. Rappaport, *Ritual and Religion in the Making of Humanity* (Cambridge: Cambridge University Press, 1999), 24.
22. See Robert J. Fogelin, *Figuratively Speaking*, 4, 89.

23. An excellent guide for such formation and catechesis is Debra Rienstra and Ron Rienstra, *Worship Words: Discipling Language for Faithful Ministry* (Grand Rapids, MI: Baker Academic, 2009).
24. See John Macquarrie, *God-Talk: An Examination of the Language and Logic of Theology* (New York: Seabury, 1979), 203. Also, Peter W. Macky, *The Centrality of Metaphors to Biblical Thought: A Method for Interpreting the Bible* (Lewiston, NY: Edwin Mellon Press, 1990), 265–297.
25. Rachel Mann, "Credo," in *A Kingdom of Love* (Manchester, UK: Carcanet, 2019), 11.
26. *The Complete Poems of Emily Dickinson*, #18.
27. The translation featured here is that of the English Language Liturgical Consultation in 1988, 14.
28. Toyohiko Kagawa, *Meditations on the Holy Spirit*, trans. Charles A. Logan (Nashville: Cokesbury Press, 1939), 102.
29. Seymour Leichman, *The Boy Who Could Sing Pictures* (Garden City, NY: Doubleday and Company, 1968), 57.
30. "Womb of Life," *All Creation Sings*, #948. Also www.hymnary.org.
31. "Source and Sovereign," *All Creation Sings*, #947. Also www.hymnary.org.
32. See the Thanksgiving at the Table "For Lent" in *Pray, Praise, and Give Thanks*, 46–47.
33. Thomas Merton, *Seasons of Celebration: Meditations on the Cycle of Liturgical Feasts* (Notre Dame, IN: Ave Maria Press, 2009), 81.

Afterword

1. For more of my liturgical prayers, see *Pray, Praise, and Give Thanks*, and for a collection of my devotional prayers, see *Blessing and Beseeching.*

INDEX OF NAMES AND SUBJECTS

INDEX OF FIGURES OF SPEECH